John E. Goodrich

Star Selections, 1876

A fresh collection of patriotic readings, in prose and poetry

John E. Goodrich

Star Selections, 1876
A fresh collection of patriotic readings, in prose and poetry

ISBN/EAN: 9783337038519

Printed in Europe, USA, Canada, Australia, Japan

Cover: Foto ©Thomas Meinert / pixelio.de

More available books at **www.hansebooks.com**

STAR SELECTIONS,

1876.

A FRESH COLLECTION OF

PATRIOTIC READINGS,

IN

PROSE AND POETRY.

BY

PROFESSOR J. E. GOODRICH.

NEW YORK:

SHELDON & COMPANY,

No. 8 MURRAY STREET.

1877.

VALUABLE SCHOOL BOOKS.

OLNEY'S ARITHMETICS.

By Prof. Edward Olney, of Michigan University, author of the following Series of Mathematics.

Olney's Pictorial Primary Arithmetic.
Olney's Elements of Arithmetic.

These two books form a Complete Series for Common Schools, and are believed to be the cheapest and best ever published.

These Arithmetics are fresh and attractive to both teacher and scholar. The Pictorial Primary Arithmetic is most beautifully illustrated by pictures which are object lessons and not mere ornaments. It is especially adapted to our Primary Schools, and furnishes model exercises on every subject. The Elements of Arithmetic is a practical treatise, furnishing in one book all the arithmetic compatible with a well-balanced Common School Course.

PATTERSON'S SPELLERS.

Patterson's Common School Speller.
Patterson's Speller and Analyzer and School Etymology, for Advanced Classes, (two books in one.)
Patterson's Exercise Books, small size, stiff paper covers, for use with the Spellers.
Patterson's Exercise Books, large size, board covers.

We spell as we write. Patterson's Spellers are the best and most carefully arranged of any yet published. They have the choicest selection of words. Just those which the scholar ought to learn. They have practical rules for Spelling. They are especially adapted to written lessons. The arrangement is perfect. Compare them with any others published, before selecting.

THE CENTENNIAL SERIES OF SPELLING BLANKS.

They can be used with any Spellers. They are the cheapest and best Series of Blanks yet published. Have all the rules and models for written spelling.

No. 1. Words.
No. 2. Words and Definitions.
No. 3. Words, Definitions and Sentences.

THE
STAR SELECTIONS.

CENTENNIAL HYMN.

JOHN GREENLEAF WHITTIER.

OUR fathers' God ! from out whose hand
The centuries fall like grains of sand,
We meet to-day, united, free,
And loyal to our land and thee,
To thank thee for the era done,
And trust thee for the opening one.

Here, where of old, by thy design,
The fathers spake that word of thine
Whose echo is the glad refrain
Of rended bolt and falling chain,
To grace our festal time, from all
The zones of earth our guests we call.

For art and labor met in truce,
For beauty made the bride of use,
We thank thee ; but, withal, we crave
The austere virtues strong to save,
The honor proof to place or gold,
The manhood never bought or sold.

Oh ! make thou us, through centuries long,
In peace secure, in justice strong ;
Around our gift of freedom draw
The safeguards of thy righteous law ;
And, cast in some diviner mold,
Let the new cycle shame the old.

Sung at Philadelphia, July 4th, 1876.

THE OPENING CENTURY.

WILLIAM M. EVARTS.

THE spirit of the nation is at the highest ; its triumph over the inborn, inbred perils of the Constitution has chased away all fears, justified all hopes, and with universal joy we greet this day. We have not proved unworthy of a great ancestry ; we have had the virtue to uphold what they so wisely, so firmly established. With these proud possessions of the past, with powers matured, with principles settled, with habits formed, the nation passes, as it were, from preparatory growth to responsible development of character, and the steady performance of duty. What labors await it, what trials shall attend it, what triumphs for human nature, what glory for itself, are prepared for this people in the coming century, we may not assume to foretell. " One generation passeth away, and another generation cometh, but the earth abideth forever," and we reverently hope that these our constituted liberties shall be maintained to the unending line of our posterity, and so long as the earth itself shall endure.

In the great procession of nations, in the great march of humanity, we hold our place. Peace is our duty, peace is our policy. In its arts, its labors, and its victories, then, we find scope for all our energies, rewards for all our ambitions, renown enough for all our love and fame. In the august presence of so many nations, which, by their representatives, have done us the honor to be witnesses of our commemorative joy and gratulation, and in sight of the collected evidences of the greatness of their own civilization with which they grace our celebration, we may well confess how much we fall short, how much we have to make up, in the emulative competitions of the times. Yet, even in this presence, and with a just deference to the age, the power, the greatness of the other nations of the earth, we do not fear to appeal to the opinion of mankind whether, as we point to our land, our people, and our laws, the contemplation should not inspire us with a lover's enthusiasm for our country.

Time makes no pauses in his march. Even while I speak the last hour of the receding is replaced by the first hour of the coming century, and reverence for the past gives way to the joys and hopes, the activities and the responsibilities of the future. A hundred years hence, the piety of that generation will recall the ancestral glory which we celebrate to-day, and crown it with the plaudits of a vast population which no man can number. . By the mere circumstance of this periodicity our generation will be in the minds, in the hearts, on the lips of our countrymen, at the next centennial commemoration, in comparison with their own character and condition, and with the great founders of the nation. What shall they say of us ? How shall they estimate the part we bear in the unbroken line of the nation's progress ? And so on in the long reach of time, forever and forever, our place in the secular roll of the ages must always bring us into observation and criticism. Under this double trust, then, from the past and for the future, let us take heed to our ways, and while it is called to-day, resolve that the great heritage we have received shall be handed down through the long line of the advancing generations, the home of liberty, the abode of justice, the stronghold of faith among men, " which holds the moral elements of the world together," and of faith in God, which binds that world to his throne.—*From Oration at Philadelphia, July 4th, 1876.*

CENTENNIAL HYMN.

OLIVER WENDELL HOLMES.

BRIGHT on the banners of lily and rose,
  Lo, the last sun of our century sets !
Wreath the black cannon that scowled on our foes.
  All but her friendships the Nation forgets !
  All but her friends and their welcome forgets.
These are around her, but where are her foes ?
  Lo, while the sun of her century sets,
Peace with her garlands of lily and rose.

1 *

Welcome ! a shout like the war-trumpet's swell
  Wakes the wild echoes that slumber around.
Welcome ! it quivers from Liberty's bell ;
  Welcome ! the walls of her temple resound ;
  Hark ! the grey walls of her temple resound.
Fade the far voices o'er hillside and dell ;
  Welcome ! still whisper the echoes around ;
Welcome ! still trembles on Liberty's bell.

Thrones of the Continents, Isles of the Sea,
  Yours are the garlands of peace we entwine.
Welcome, once more, to the land of the free,
  Shadowed alike by the palm and the pine ;
  Softly they murmur, the palm and the pine.
Hushed is our strife in the land of the free ;
  Over your children their branches entwine,
Thrones of the Continents, Isles of the Sea.

  Sung at Philadelphia, July 4th, 1876.

A SONG OF A CENTURY.

WASHINGTON GLADDEN.

A HUNDRED times the harvesters have reaped the golden
  grain,
A hundred times the snow have heaped the mountain and
  the plain,
And the mayflowers and the roses have bloomed a hundred
  times,
Since that good day whose deeds I sing in these my simple
  rhymes.

True men were they who met that day as spoke the English
  tongue,
Good Saxon men, who loved the land from whence their sires
  had sprung ;
Heirs of all sacred lore of fame that English lips can teach,
Heirs of all precious things that live in our old English speech.

The land that bore them spurned their love ; the hand that
    should have fed,
Across the sea, with kingly scorn, had sent them stones for
    bread ;
And, breaking now the bonds that fast to manacles have
    grown,
They fling their homage boldly down before Old England's
    throne :—

" Laws that we may not help to make we never will obey ;
Dues that we must not help to fix are dues we will not pay.
This land is ours. We'll rule this land. No monarch o'er
    the sea
Shall make us serve ; for right is ours, and might to make
    us free."

To this clear word, so bravely said, these plain men put their
    hands,
And pledge to it, in face of Heaven, their faith, their lives,
    their lands.
" Ring !" cries the listening bellman's boy. " Ring ! for the
    deed is done ! "
Swift with the word, O couriers fleet, to all the cities run !

East, west, north, south, the tidings speed ; bells ring and
    bonfires burn ;
The whole land hails the challenge with a courage high and
    stern ;
In camp and field the soldier grasps the firelock by his side,
Remembering that the brave of earth for liberty have died.

The farmer hears the summons and forsakes the growing
    grain ;
The merchant locks his counting-room ; the joiner drops his
    plane ;
The lawyer leaves his suit untried ; the scribe throws down
    his scroll ;
All quick to write their names upon their country's muster-
    roll.

What need to tell the tale of blood—of battle, siege, campaign ;
Of Trenton, Princeton, Brandywine, and Yorktown o'er
    again ;
Of Molly Stark's good man who drove the Hessians from the
    height ?
Of old Mad Anthony's storming of the Stony Point at night ;

Of Put's rash gallop down the rocks ; of Allen's morning-call ;
Of Marion's rangers in the swamps ; of Arnold's mournful
    fall ;
Of all the work our fathers wrought, the hardships that they
    bore ;—
Their deeds, their names are household words, and shall be
    evermore.

We know these men were made, like us, in molds of common
    clay ;
Though even as demigods they loom through history's morn-
    ing gray.
We know that hate and spite and greed defiled their holiest
    things ;
Yet thankful Love doth hide their faults beneath her shining
    wings.

For still they kept, through bitter years, good faith with
    Liberty,
Nor sparing toil nor counting cost to make their country free.
And here, to-day, with reverent words and praising hearts we
    stand,
To own the debt we owe the men who saved for us this land.

A hundred years ! 'Tis quickly said. But who shall gauge the
    time,
Or think to span with straining speech this century sublime ?
Whose pencil, dipped in light, can trace the nation's bright-
    ening way,
From the dim dawn of liberty to this illustrious day ?

Westward the teeming millions reach, o'er mountain and
 o'er plain ;
The prairie blooms are swept from sight by billowy tides of
 grain ;
By river, lake, and main upspring a hundred cities grand ;
And commerce spins her robe of steel and spreads it o'er the
 land.

Onward the legions press o'er paths by none but wild men
 trod,
Making across the desert lands a highway for their God,
Girding the east and west together, till, from sea to sea,
The nation belts the continent—puissant, prosperous, free !

Free ! but the word on many an ear strikes like a solemn bell,
Tolling the knell of heroes who for Freedom fought and fell ;
For God, who counts the tears and groans and bloody sweat
 of slaves,
Hath summed the direful reckoning up, and lo ! a million
 graves !

A million graves ! deep furrows plowed by God's avenging
 might !
But from such planting what shall grow in this new morning's
 light ?
O husbandmen of liberty ! be watchful and be wise !
The greed of gold, the lust of power, the sorcery of lies,

Grow thick and rank in soil that late with martyrs' blood was
 red,
And choke the seed they died to sow, our own heroic dead !
Now, by the love ye bear them, pluck the vileness from the
 land,
Till, east and west, truth, freedom, peace in golden harvests
 stand.

                                        —*The Independent.*

OUR CENTENNIAL CELEBRATION

ORESTES CLEVELAND.

FELLOW-COMMISSIONERS :—When we were welcomed in Independence Hall, and again in visiting old Carpenter's Hall, I was impressed with the grand and glorious memories clustering round about Philadelphia, all pointing with solemn significance to the occasion we are preparing to celebrate. No such family gathering has ever been known in the world's history, and we shall have passed away and been forgotten when the next one recurs.

The vast and varied and marvelous results of inventive industry from all the world shall gather here. And it is fitting ; for here, upon this continent, in this new country, under the fostering care of the wise and beneficent provisions of our patent laws, the inventive genius of the age finds her most congenial home. From the International Exhibition of 1876 the education of skilled labor, in this country at least, is to take a new departure.

Here will be spread out before us the manufactures of Great Britain, the source of all her power. From France will come articles of taste and utility, exquisite in design and perfect in execution. From Russia, iron and leather no nation has yet learned to produce. From Berlin and Munich, artistic productions in iron and bronze. From Switzerland, her unequaled wood-carvings and delicate watch-work. From Bohemia shall come the perfection of glass-blowing, and musical instruments from the Black Forest.

From the people of poor old Spain, to whose daring and public spirit nearly four centuries back we owe the possibilities of this hour, shall come the evidences of a foretime greatness, now unhappily faded away for want of education amongst the mass of her people. From Nineveh and Pompeii the evidences of a buried past. From China, her curious workmanship, the result of accumulated ingenuity reaching back beyond the time when history began. Matchless wood-work from Japan, and from far India her treasures rare and wonderful. Turkey and Persia shall bring their gorgeous fabrics to diversify and stimulate our taste. The Queen of the East, passing the Suez Canal, shall cross the great deep and bow her turbaned head to this young giant of the West, and he shall point her people to the source of his vast powers—the education of all the people.

One of our noted orators laid before us the other night such evidence as he could gather of the lost arts of the ancients, and he demands to know what we have to compensate us for the loss. I claim that we have produced some things, even in this new country, worthy of that orator's notice. Instead of tearing open the bosom of mother earth with the root of a tree, as the ancients did, that we may feed upon the bounties of nature, the green sward rolls away with the perfection and grace of art itself from the polished molding-board of the Pittsburg steel plow. Machinery casts abroad the seed, and a reaping-machine gathers the harvest. Whitney's cotton-gin prepares the fiber; Lyall's positive-motion loom takes the place of the old wheel; and a sewing machine fits the fabric for the use of man. What had the ancients, I demand to know, that could compensate them for the want of these American inventions? I do not speak of the American telegraph, or of the power of steam, though we have done more than all other nations together in developing its possibilities. The Magi of the East, in their wildest frenzy of imagination, never dreamed of the wonders of these!—*From a speech at the preliminary session of the Centennial Commission.*

HOSPES CIVITATIS.

Annus Mirabilis Reipublicæ MDCCCLXXVI.

RICHARD HENRY STODDARD.

VICTORIOUS in her senate-house she stands,
    Mighty among the nations, latest born ;
Armed men stood round her cradle, violent hands
    Were laid upon her, and her limbs were torn ;

Yet she arose, and turned upon her foes,
And, beaten down, arose,
Grim, as who goes to meet
And grapple with Defeat,
And pull Destruction from her iron seat !
When saw the Earth another,
O valorous Daughter of imperious Mother !
Who greatly dared as thou ?
Making thy land one wide Thermopylæ,
＊ And the long leagues of sea thy Salamis,
Determined to be free
As the unscaled heaven is,
Whose calm is in thy eyes, whose stars are on thy brow !

Thy children gathered round thee to defend,
O mother of a race of hardy sons !
Left plows to rust in the furrows, snatched their guns,
And rode hot haste as though to meet a friend,
Who might be nigh his end,
Which *thou* wert not, though often sore beset ;
Nor did they fall in vain who fell for thee ;
Nor could thy enemies, though its roots they wet
With thy best blood, destroy thy glorious tree,
That on its stem of greatness flowers late :
Hedged with sharp spines it shot up year by year,
As if the planets drew it to their sphere,
The quick earth spouting sap through all its veins ;
Till, of the days that wait
To see it burst in bloom, not one remains ;
Not so much as an hour ;
For lo ! it is in flower—
Bourgeoned, full blown in an instant ! Tree of trees,
The fame whereof has flown across the seas ;
Whereat the elder sisters of the race
Have hastened to these high walls,
These populous halls,

To look on this Centurial Tree,
And to strike hands with thee,
And see thy happy millions face to face !

Welcome, a thousand welcomes ! Our emotion
  Demands a speech we have not : it demands
The unutterable largeness of the ocean,
  The immeasurable broadness of the lands
That own us masters. Who is he shall speak
This language for us ? from what mountain peak ?
And in the rhythms of what epic song,
    At once serene and strong ?
Welcomes, ten thousand welcomes ! It is much,
  O Sisters ! ye have done in coming here ;
    For, from the hour ye touch
Our peaceful shores, ye are peaceful, equal, dear !
    Not with exultations,
    O Sister, Mother nations !
Do we receive your coming ; for more than many see
Comes with ye ; do ye see it ? It is what is to be
Some day among your myriads, who will no more obey ;
But, peaceable or warring, will then find out the way
  Themselves to govern : if they tolerate
  Kaisers, and Kings, and Princelings, as to-day,
    It will be because they pity and are too good to hate.
The New World is teaching the Old World to be free :
  This, her acknowledgment from these, is more
    Than all that went before :
Henceforth, America, Man looks up to thee
  Not down at the dead Republics ! Rise, arise !
    That all men may behold thee. Be not proud ;
      Be humble and be wise ;
    And let thy head be bowed
  To the Unknown, Supreme One, who on high
    Has willed thee not to die !
    Be grateful, watchful, brave ;

See that among thy children none shall plunder,
Nor rend asunder ;
Swift to detect and punish, and strong to shield and save !
Shall the drums beat, trumpets sound,
And the cannon thunder round ?
No ; these are warlike noises, and must cease.
Not thus, while the whole world from battle rests,
The Commonwealth receives her honored guests ;
She celebrates no triumphs but of peace.

—*Scribner's Magazine.*

MISSION AND DESTINY OF THE UNITED STATES.

PROFESSOR HUXLEY.

I HAVE often been struck in England with the charm which Americans seem to feel in visiting those ancient cities of ours, or climbing the battlements of crumbling castles, the names of which are inseparably associated with the great epochs of our noble literature, or with the various steps of that blood-stained progress by which the savage Briton or the wild pirate of the North Sea has become converted into a champion of order, a chief means of the progress of civilization. It is impossible to be otherwise—as an Englishman—than in entire sympathy with a feeling of this kind ; but if retrospect has its charm, I think it is no less true that there is a joy in anticipation ; and to an Englishman who first lands upon your shores, who finds himself traveling for hundreds of miles through what I can only call strings of great cities, who even in the roughest way compares the extent of your territory with that which he has left, and looks at your marvelous resources in everything that tends to the welfare and riches of mankind, there is a something sublime in the vista of the future.

I don't say this with the least intention of flattering that particular vulgar sentiment which is commonly called national pride. On the contrary, I don't know that I have any particular respect for bigness as such or for wealth as such :

and most assuredly bigness is not the same thing as greatness, and territory does not constitute a nation. What I referred to just now as the issue which had suggested itself to me, fraught, as I will say again, with a certain sublimity, a terror as of overhanging fate, is the question : What are you going to do with all these things ? To what purpose will you put this great store of material wealth and this vast amount of human intelligence and capacity which is among you to deal with ? The question is one which, it seems to me, nó man has a chance of answering with the remotest probability at the present moment.

You are undertaking the greatest political experiment that has ever been performed by any people whatever. You are at this present centenary a nation of forty millions of people. At your next centenary rational and probable expectation may look to see you two hundred millions, and you have before you the problem whether two hundred millions of English-speaking, strong-willed people will be able to hold together under the form of republican institutions and under the real despotism of universal suffrage ; whether State rights will hold their own against the necessary centralization of a great nation, if it is to act as a whole, or whether centralization will gain the day without breaking down republican institutions. The territory you cover is as large as Europe, as diverse in climate as England and Spain, as France and Russia ; and you have to see whether, with the diversity of interests, mercantile and other, which arise under these circumstances, national ties will be stronger than the tendency to separation. As you grow in numbers and the pressure of population makes itself manifest, the specter of pauperism will stalk among you, and you will be very unlike Europe if communism and socialism do not claim to be heard.

I cannot imagine that any one should envy you this great destiny—for a great destiny it is to solve these problems some way or other. Great will be your honor, great will be your position, if you solve them righteously and honestly ; great your shame and your misery it you fail. But let me express my most strong conviction that the key to success, the essential condition to success, is one and one only : that it rests entirely upon the intellectual clearness and upon the moral worth of the individual citizen. Education cannot give intellectual clearness, it cannot give moral worth, but it may cherish them and bring them to the front ; and, in that sense, the university may be and ought to be the fortress of the higher life of the nation.—*From address at opening of Johns Hopkins University, Baltimore, Sept. 12th, 1876.*

THE CENTENNIAL CANTATA.

SIDNEY LANIER, OF GEORGIA.

FROM this hundred-terraced height
Sight more large, with nobler light,
Ranges down yon towering years :
Humbler smiles and lordlier tears
Shine and fall, shine and fall ;
While old voices rise and call
Yonder, where the to-and-fro
Weltering of my Long-ago
Moves about the moveless base
Far below my resting-place.

Mayflower, Mayflower, slowly hither flying,
Trembling westward o'er yon balking sea ;
Hearts within 'Farewell, dear England,' sighing,
Winds without ' But dear in vain' replying,
Gray-lipp'd waves about thee shouted, crying
          ' No ! It shall not be ! '

Jamestown, out of thee—
Plymouth, thee—thee, Albany—
Winter cries, ' Ye freeze : away ! '
Fever cries, ' Ye burn : away ! '
Hunger cries, ' Ye starve : away ! '
Vengeance cries, ' Your graves shall stay ! '

Then old Shapes and Masks of Things,
Framed like Faiths or clothed like Kings ;
Ghosts of Goods, once fleshed and fair,
Grown foul Bads in alien air ;
War, and his most noisy lords,
Tongued with lithe and poisoned swords ;
  Error, Terror, Rage, and Crime,
  All in a windy night of time
  Cried to me from land and sea,
    ' No ! Thou shalt not be !'

          Hark !

Huguenots whispering Yea in the dark !
Puritans whispering Yea in the dark !
Yea, like an arrow shot true to his mark,
Darts through the tyrannous heart of Denial,
Patience and Labor and solemn-souled Trial,
      Foiled, still beginning,
      Soiled, but not sinning,
Toil through the stertorous death of the Night,
Toil, when wild brother-wars new dark the Light,
Toil and forgive and kiss o'er and replight.

    Now, praise to God's oft-granted grace,
    Now, praise to Man's undaunted face,
    Despite the land, despite the sea,
    I was, I am, and I shall be.
How long, good Angel, oh ! how long ?
Sing me from heaven a man's own song !

    " Long as thine Art shall love true love ;
      Long as thy Science truth shall know ;
    Long as thine Eagle harms no Dove ;
      Long as thy Law by law shall grow ;
    Long as thy God is God above ;
      Thy brother every man below ;

So long, dear land of all my love,
    Thy name shall shine, thy fame shall glow !"

O Music, from this height of time my Word unfold :
In thy large signals all men's hearts Man's Heart behold :
Mid-heaven unroll thy chords as friendly flags unfurled,
And wave the world's best lover's welcome to the world.
            —Sung at Philadelphia, July 4th, 1876.

THE PRESENT NOT INFERIOR TO THE PAST IN RESPECT TO VIRTUE AND PATRIOTISM.

RICHARD S. STORRS, D. D.

I SCOUT the thought that we, as a people, are worse than our fathers ! John Adams, at the head of the War Department, in 1776, wrote bitter laments of the corruption which existed in even that infant age of the Republic, and of the spirit of venality, rapacious and insatiable, which was then the most alarming enemy of America. He declared himself ashamed of the age he lived in ! In Jefferson's day all Federalists expected the universal dominion of French infidelity. In Jackson's day all Whigs thought the country gone to ruin already, as if Mr. Biddle had had the entire public hope locked up in the vaults of his terminated bank. In Polk's day the excitements of the Mexican War gave life and germination to all seeds of rascality. There has never been a time—not here alone, in any country—when the fierce light of incessant inquiry blazing on men in public life would not have brought out such forces of evil as we have seen, or when the condemnation which followed the discovery would have been sharper. And it is among my deepest convictions that, with all which has happened to debase and debauch it, the nation at large was never before more mentally vigorous or morally sound than it is to-day.

When the war of 1861 broke on the land, and shadowed every home within it, this city—which had voted, by immense majorities, against the existing administration, and which was linked by a million ties with the great communities that were rushing to assail it—flung out its banners from window and spire, from City Hall and newspaper office, and poured its wealth and life into the service of sustaining the Government, with a swiftness and strength and a vehement energy that were never surpassed. When, afterward, greedy and treacherous men, capable and shrewd, deceiving the unwary, hiring the skillful, and molding the very law to their uses, had concentrated in their hands the government of the city, and had bound it in seemingly invincible chains while they plundered its treasury; it rose upon them, when advised of the facts, as Samson rose upon the Philistines; and the two new cords that were upon his hands no more suddenly became as flax that was burned, than did those manacles imposed upon the city by the craft of the Ring.

Its leaders of opinion to-day are the men whom virtue exalts and character crowns. It rejoices in a Chief Magistrate as upright and intrepid in a virtuous course as any of those whom he succeeds. It is part of a State whose present position, in laws and officers and the spirit of its people, does no discredit to the noblest of its memories. And from these heights between the rivers, looking over the land, looking out on the earth to which its daily embassies go, it sees nowhere beneath the sun a city more ample in its moral securities, a city more dear to those who possess it, a city more splendid in promise and in hope.— *From oration at New York, July 4th, 1876.*

AMERICA.—AN ODE.

BAYARD TAYLOR.

FORESEEN in the vision of sages,
  Foretold when martyrs bled,
She was born of the longing of ages,
  By the truth of the noble dead
  And the faith of the living fed !
No blood in her lightest veins
Frets at remembered chains,

Nor shame of bondage has bowed her head.
  In her form and features still
  The unblenching Puritan will,
  Cavalier honor, Huguenot grace,
  The Quaker truth and sweetness,
And the strength of the danger-girdled race
Of Holland, blend in a proud completeness.
From the homes of all, where her being began,
  She took what she gave to Man :
  Justice, that knew no station,
    Belief, as soul decreed,
  Free air for aspiration,
Free force for independent deed !
  She takes, but to give again,
As the sea returns the rivers in rain ;
And gathers the chosen of her seed
From the hunted of every crown and creed.
Her Germany dwells by a gentler Rhine ;
Her Ireland sees the old sunburst shine ;
Her France pursues some dream divine ;
Her Norway keeps his mountain pine ;
Her Italy waits by the western brine ;
  And broad-based under all,
Is planted England's oaken-hearted mood,
  As rich in fortitude
As e'er went worldward from the island-wall !
  Fused in her candid light,
To one strong race all races here unite :
Tongues melt in hers, hereditary foemen
Forget their sword and slogankith and clan ;
  'Twas glory, once, to be a Roman ;
She makes it glory, now, to be a Man !

    Behold ! she bendeth now,
Humbling the chaplet of her hundred years.
There is a solemn sweetness on her brow,
  And in her eyes are sacred tears.

Can she forget,
In present joy, the burden of her debt,
When for a captive race
She grandly staked and won
The total promise of her power begun,
And bared her bosom's grace
To the sharp wound that inly tortures yet?
Can she forget
The million graves her young devotion set,
The hands that clasp above
From either side, in sad, returning love?
Can she forget—
Here, where the Ruler of to-day,
The Citizen of to-morrow,
And equal thousands to rejoice and pray
Beside these holy walls are met—
Her birth-cry, mixed of keenest bliss and sorrow?
Where, on July's immortal morn
Held forth, the people saw her head,
And shouted to the world: "The King is dead,
But lo! the Heir is born!"
When fire of Youth, and sober trust of Age,
In Farmer, Soldier, Priest, and Sage,
Arose and cast upon her
Baptismal garments—never robes so fair
Clad prince in Old-world air—
Their lives, their fortunes, and their sacred honor!

Arise! Recrown thy head,
Radiant with blessing of the Dead!
Bear from this hallowed place
The prayer that purifies thy lips,
The light of courage that defies eclipse,
The rose of Man's new morning on thy face!
Let no iconoclast
Invade thy rising Pantheon of the Past,

2

To make a blank where Adams stood,
To touch the Father's sheathed and sacred blade,
Spoil crowns on Jefferson and Franklin laid,
Or wash from Freedom's feet the stain of Lincoln's
    blood !
    Hearken, as from that haunted hall
        Their voices call :
    " We lived and died for thee :
We greatly dared that thou might'st be ;
    So, from thy children still
We claim denials which at last fulfill,
And freedom yielded to preserve thee free !
    Beside clear-hearted Right,
That smiles at Power's uplifted rod,
    Plant Duties that requite,
And Order that sustains, upon thy sod,
    And stand in stainless might
Above all self, and only less than God ! "

    O sacred Woman-Form !
Of the first People's need and passion wrought,
    No thin, pale ghost of Thought,
But fair as Morning and as heart's-blood warm,
Wearing thy priestly tiar on Judah's hills ;
Clear-eyed beneath Athené's helm of gold ;
    Or from Rome's central seat
Hearing the pulses of the Continents beat
    In thunder where her legions rolled ;
Compact of high heroic hearts and wills,
    Whose being circles all
The selfless aims of man, and all fulfills ;
Thyself not free, so long as one is thrall ;
    Goddess, that as a Nation lives,
    And as a Nation dies,
That for her children as a man defies,
And to her children as a mother gives—

Take our fresh fealty now !
No more a Chieftainess, with wampum-zone
And feather-cinctured brow ;
No more a new Britannia, grown
To spread an equal banner to the breeze,
And lift thy trident o'er the double seas ;
But, with unborrowed crest,
In thine own native beauty dressed—
The front of pure command, the unflinching eye, thine
own !

Look up, look forth, and on !
There's light in the dawning sky ;
The clouds are parting, the night is gone :
Prepare for the work of the day !
Fallow thy pastures lie
And far thy shepherds stray,
And the fields of thy vast domain
Are waiting for purer seed
Of knowledge, desire, and deed ;
For keener sunshine and mellower rain !
But keep thy garments pure ;
Pluck them back, with the old disdain,
From touch of the hands that stain !
So shall thy strength endure.
Transmute into good the gold of gain,
Compel to beauty thy ruder powers,
Till the bounty of coming hours
Shall plant, on thy fields apart,
With the oak of Toil, the rose of Art !
Be watchful, and keep us so :
Be strong, and fear no foe :
Be just, and the world shall know !
With the same love love us, as we give ;
And the day shall never come
That finds us weak or dumb

To join and smite and cry
In the great task, for thee to die,
And the greater task, for thee to live !
—*Read at Philadelphia, July 4th, 1876.* [*Abridged.*]

———•———

THE AIMS AND EXAMPLES OF THE FATHERS.

CHARLES DEVENS, JR.

FELLOW CITIZENS : We stand to-day on a great battle-field in honor of the patriotism and valor of those who fought upon it. · It is the step which they made in the world's history we would seek to commemorate ; it is the example which they have offered us we would seek to imitate. The wise and thoughtful men who directed this controversy knew well that it is by the wars that personal ambition has stimulated, by the armies whose force has ‘been wielded alike for domestic oppression or foreign conquest, that the sway of despots has been so widely maintained. They had no love for war or any of its works, but they were more ready to meet its dangers in their attachment to the cause of civil and religious liberty. They desired to found no Roman republic, “ whose banners, fanned by conquest's crimson wing,” should float victorious over prostrate nations; but one where the serene beauty of the arts of peace should put to shame the strifes that have impoverished peoples and degraded nations. To-day let us rejoice in the liberty which they have gained for us ; but let no utterances but those of peace salute our ears, no thoughts but those of peace animate our hearts.

Above the plains of Marathon, even now, as the Grecian shepherd watches over his flocks, he fancies that the skies sometimes are filled with lurid light, and that in the clouds above are re-enacted the scenes of that great day when, on the field below, Greece maintained her freedom against the hordes which had assailed her. Again seem to come in long array, rich with “ barbaric pearl and gold,” the turbaned ranks of the Persian host, and the air is filled with the clang of sword and shield, as again the fiery Greek seems to throw himself upon and drive before him his foreign invader ; shadows though they all are, that flit in wild, confused masses along the spectral sky.

Above the field where we stand, even in the wildest dream, may no such scenes offend the calmness of the upper air ; but may the stars look forever down upon prosperity and peace ; upon the bay studded with its white-winged ships ; upon the populous and far-extending city, with its marts of commerce, its palaces of industry, its temples where each man may worship according to his own conscience ; and, as the continent shall pass beneath their steady rays, may the millions of happy homes attest a land where the benign influence of free government has brought happiness and contentment, where labor is rewarded, where manhood is honored, and where virtue and religion are revered.—*From the Centennial Oration pronounced in Charlestown, Mass., June 17th, 1875.*

———

CENTENNIAL HYMN.

W. A. MUHLENBERG, D.D.

GIVE praise, all ye people, give praise to the Lord ;
Alleluias of freedom let freemen accord ;
Let the East and the West, North and South, roll along
Sea, mountain, and prairie one jubilant song.

    Give praise, all ye people, give praise to the Lord ;
    Alleluias of freedom let freemen accord.

For the sunshine and rainfall, again and again
Our myriads of acres enriching with grain ;
For the earth still unloading her manifold wealth ;
For the skies beaming vigor, the winds breathing health.

               Give praise, etc.

For the nation's wide table, so bounteously spread
That the many have feasted, and all have been fed,
With no bondage their God-given rights to enthrall,
But liberty, guarded by justice for all.

                       Give praise, etc.

Ye sons of the anvil, the loom, and the plow,—
His the mines and the fields ; to him gratefully bow.
His the flocks and the herds ; sing on hillsides and vales ;
On his ocean domain chant his name with the gales.

                       Give praise, etc.

Ye merchantmen princes, your riches behold,
The largess of him whose the silver and gold ;
And ye, too, renowned in art, science, and lore,
His glory in all be it yours to adore.

                       Give praise, etc.

Brave men of our forces, lifeguard of our coasts,
To your leader aye loyal, Jehovah of Hosts,
Glow the stars on your banners, reflecting his light,
Your conflicts alone for the Good, True, and Right.

                       Give praise, etc.

Now praise we again for the Union ; it stands
Unchanged as it came from our forefathers' hands,
A century gone.   Oh, with praise blend the prayer ;
Gracious Lord, centuries more be the Union thy care.

  Give praise, all ye people, give praise to the Lord ;
Alleluias of freedom let freemen accord.

                     —Christian Intelligencer.

THE PRESENT AND THE FUTURE OF AMERICA.

HENRY ARMITT BROWN.

WHAT is it, countrymen, that we need to-day? Wealth? Behold it in your hands. Power? God has given it you. Liberty? It is your birthright. Peace? It dwells amongst you. You have a government founded in the hearts of men, built by the people for the common good. You have a land flowing with milk and honey; your homes are happy, your workshops busy, your barns are full. The school, the railway, the telegraph, the printing-press, have welded you together into one. Descend those mines that honeycomb the hills! Behold that commerce whitening every sea! Stand by yon gates and see that multitude pour through them from the corners of the earth, grafting the qualities of older stocks upon one stem, mingling the blood of many races in a common stream, and swelling the rich volume of our English speech with varied music from a hundred tongues! You have a long and glorious history, a past glittering with heroic deeds, an ancestry full of lofty and imperishable examples. You have passed through danger, endured privation, been acquainted with sorrow, been tried by suffering. You have journeyed in safety through the wilderness and crossed in triumph the Red Sea of civil strife, and the foot of Him who led you hath not faltered, nor the light of His countenance been turned away.

The century that is opening is all our own. The years that lie before us are a virgin page. We can inscribe them as we will. The future of our country rests upon us; the happiness of posterity depends upon us. The fate of humanity may be in our hands. That pleading voice, choked with the sobs of ages, which has so often spoken to deaf ears, is lifted up to us. It asks us to be brave, benevolent, consistent, true to the teachings of our history, proving "divine descent by worth divine." It asks us to be virtuous—building up public virtue by private worth; seeking that righteousness which exalteth nations. It asks us to be pa-

triotic—loving our country before all other things ; her happiness our happiness, her honor our honor, her fame our own.
It asks us, in the name of justice, in the name of charity, in
the name of freedom, in the name of God.

The American Union hath endured a hundred years !
Here, on this threshold of the future, the voice of humanity
shall not plead to us in vain.   There will be darkness in the
days to come ; danger for our courage ; temptation for our
virtue ; doubt for our faith ; suffering for our fortitude.   A
thousand shall fall before us, and tens of thousands at our
right hand.   The years shall pass beneath our feet, and
century follow century in quick succession.   The generations
of men shall come and go ; the greatness of yesterday shall
be forgotten ; to-day and the glories of this noon shall vanish
before to-morrow's sun.   Yet America shall not perish, but
endure while the spirit of our fathers animates their sons.—
*From the Oration delivered on the Centennial Anniversary
of the meeting of the First Continental Congress.*

A HUNDRED YEARS FROM NOW.

THE surging sea of human life forever onward rolls,
And bears to the eternal shore its daily freight of souls.
Though bravely sails our bark to-day, pale death sits at the
    prow,
And few shall know we ever lived a hundred years from
    now.

O mighty human brotherhood ! why fiercely war and strive,
While God's great world has ample space for everything
    alive ?
Broad fields, uncultured and unclaimed, are waiting for the
    plow
Of progress that shall make them bloom a hundred years from
    now.

Why should we try so earnestly, in life's short, narrow span,
On golden stairs to climb so high above our fellow-man ?
Why blindly at an earthly shrine in slavish homage bow ?
Our gold will rust, ourselves be dust, a hundred years from
  now.

Why prize so much the world's applause, why dread so much
  its blame?
A fleeting echo is its voice of censure or of fame ;
The praise that thrills the heart, the scorn that dyes with
  shame the brow,
Will be as long-forgotten dreams a hundred years from now.

O patient hearts that meekly bear your weary load of wrong !
O earnest hearts that bravely dare, and striving grow more
  strong !
Press on till perfect peace is won ; you'll never dream of how
You struggled o'er life's thorny road a hundred years from
  now.

Grand, lofty souls, who live and toil, that freedom, right, and
  truth
Alone may rule the universe, for you is endless youth ;
When 'mid the blest with God you rest, the grateful lands
  shall bow
Above your clay in reverent love a hundred years from now.

Our Father, to whose sleepless eyes the past and future stand
An open page, like babes we cling to thy protecting hand ;
Change, sorrow, death are naught to us, if we may safely bow
Beneath the shadow of thy throne a hundred years from now.

                    —*New Orleans Morning Star.*

2*

WASHINGTON AND NAPOLEON.

CHARLES FRANCIS ADAMS.

WASHINGTON, as I understand him, was gifted with nothing ordinarily defined as genius, and he had not had great advantages of education. His intellectual powers were clear, but not much above the average men of his time. What knowledge he possessed had been gained from association with others in his long public career, rather than by secluded study. As an orator he scarcely distinguished himself by more than one brilliant stroke ; as a writer, the greater part of his correspondence discloses nothing more than average natural good sense ; and on the field of battle his powers pale before the splendid strategy of Napoleon Bonaparte.

Yet, notwithstanding all these deductions, the thread of his life from youth to age displays a maturity of judgment, a consistency of principle, a steadiness of action, a discriminating wisdom, and a purity of purpose hardly found united to the same extent in any other instance I can recall in history. Of his entire disinterestedness in all his pecuniary relations with the public it is needless for me to speak. More than all, and above all, he was always master of himself. If there be one quality more than another in his character which may exercise a useful control over the men of the present hour, it is the total disregard of self, when in the most elevated positions for influence and example.

The star of Napoleon was just rising to its zenith as that of Washington passed away. In point of military genius, Napoleon probably equaled if he did not exceed any person known in history. In regard to the direction of the interests of a nation he may have occupied a very high place. He inspired an energy and a vigor in the veins of the French people which they sadly needed after the demoralizing sway of centuries of Bourbon kings. With even a smaller modicum of the wisdom so prominent in Washington, he too might have left a people to honor his memory down to the latest times. But it was not to be. Do you ask the reason ? It is this :

His motives of action always centered in self. His example gives a warning, but not a guide. For when selfishness animates a ruler there is no cause of surprise if he sacrifice, without scruple, an entire generation of men as a holocaust to the great principle of evil, merely to maintain or extend his sway. Had Napoleon copied the example of Washington, he would have been the idol of all later generations in France. For Washington to have copied the example of Napoleon would have been simply impossible.—*From Oration at Taunton, Mass., July 4th, 1876.*

CHARACTER OF WASHINGTON.

JAMES RUSSELL LOWELL.

OH ! for a drop of that terse Roman's ink,
Who gave Agricola dateless length of days,
   To celebrate him fitly ; neither swerve
To phrase unkempt, nor pass discretion's brink,
   With him so statue-like in sad reserve,
   So diffident to claim, so forward to deserve !
Nor need I shun due influence of his fame
   Who, mortal among mortals, seemed as now
   The equestrian shape with unimpassioned brow
That paces silent on through vistas of acclaim.
What figure more immovably august
   Than that grave strength so patient and so pure,
   Calm in good fortune, when it wavered, sure ?
That soul serene, impenetrably just,
   Modeled on classic lines so simple they endure ?
   That soul so softly radiant and so white
   The track it left seems less of fire than light,
Cold but to such as love distemperature ?
   And if pure light, as some deem, be the force
   That drives rejoicing planets on their course,
   Why for his power benign seek an impurer source ?

His was the true enthusiasm that burns long,
　Domestically bright,
　Fed from itself and shy of human sight,
The hidden force that makes a lifetime strong,
And not the short-lived fuel of a song.
　Passionless, say you ?　What is passion for
But to sublime our natures and control,
To front heroic toils with late return,
　Or none, or such as shames the conqueror ?
That fire was fed with substance of the soul,
And not with holiday stubble, that could burn
　Through seven slow years of unadvancing war ;
Equal when fields were lost or fields were won,
With breath of popular applause or blame
Nor fanned nor damped, unquenchably the same,
Too inward to be reached by flaws of idle fame.
Soldier and statesman, rarest unison ;
High-poised example of great duties done
　Simply as breathing, a world's honors worn
　As life's indifferent gifts to all men born ;
Dumb for himself, unless it were to God ;
　But for his barefoot soldiers eloquent,
Tramping the snow to coral where they trod,
　Held by his awe in hollow-eyed content ;
Modest, yet firm as Nature's self ; unblamed,
Save by the men his nobler temper shamed ;
Not honored then or now because he wooed
The popular voice, but that he still withstood ;
Broad-minded, higher-souled, there is but one
Who was all this, and ours and all men's—Washington.
—*From a Poem read at the Cambridge, Mass., Centennial.*

AN ENGLISHMAN'S TRIBUTE TO WASHINGTON.

MANY inspiring words will be spoken of Washington this
Centennial year; but none finer, truer, more reverent, more
satisfactory, than those which an Englishman uttered of him

thirteen years after his death. It was William Smyth, Professor of Modern History at Cambridge, England, who, at the close of his last lecture upon the American War, said of Washington : "Whatever was the difficulty, the trial, the temptation, or the danger, there stood the soldier and the citizen, eternally the same, without fear and without reproach ; and there was the man who was not only at all times virtuous, but at all times wise. The merit of Washington by no means ceases with his campaigns ; it becomes after the peace of 1783 even more striking than before ; for the same man who, for the sake of liberty, was ardent enough to resist the power of Great Britain, and hazard everything on this side the grave, at a later period had to be temperate enough to resist the same spirit of liberty, when it was mistaking its proper objects and transgressing its appointed limits. The American Revolution was to approach him, and he was to kindle in the general flame ; the French Revolution was to reach him, and to consume but too many of his countrymen ; and his own ethereal mold, incapable of stain, was to purge off the baser fire victorious ! But all this was done. He might have been pardoned though he had failed amidst the enthusiasm of those around him, and when liberty was the delusion ; but the foundations of the moral world were shaken, and not the understanding of Washington." This, surely, is the character to contemplate and to desire in the great year that is passing. These are words that might be graven in gold over the portal of Mount Vernon.—*Harper's Magazine.*

PATER PATRIÆ.

CHARLES T. CONGDON.

How, in these later lays,
Shall we his antique valor praise—
The unconquered mind which, Fortune frowning,
Honor and Hope still guarded from despair ?
How sing that simple truth, when all were crowning

Those brows beloved, such victory could bear?
Or, when the league of black intrigue
  Calumnious whispered at his fame,
Loftiest of soul, in self contról,
  Smiled the assassins into shame?
    How sing the Spartan band
    Guided by that great hand?
    Wintry skies above them scowling,
    Wintry winds around them howling,
      Hunger gnawing out their life!
    How they faced the foe vainglorious,
    How they made defeat victorious,
And safety snatched from the unequal strife!

Thou mightiest ruler of a nation's heart!
Unsceptered king, by love alone enthroned!
Nor less a father than a monarch owned;
  Nor human less, though godlike! Yet apart
  No Pantheon holds thee! All alone thou art,
Man of the future, of the past, of now:
Illustrious the rest—immortal thou!
              —*From a Poem in N. Y. Tribune.*

ABRAHAM LINCOLN.

[Assassinated April 14th, 1865.]

ROBERT LEIGHTON, *Liverpool, England.*

"*Sic semper tyrannis!*" the assassin cried,
  As Lincoln fell. Oh, villain! who than he
  More lived to set both slave and tyrant free?
Or so enrapt with plans of freedom died,
That even the treacherous deed shall glance aside
  And do the dead man's will, by land and sea;
  Win bloodless battles, and make that to be
Which to his living mandate was denied?

Peace to that gentle heart ! the peace he sought
  For all mankind, nor for it died in vain.
Rest to the uncrowned king, who toiling, brought
  His bleeding country through the dreadful reign ;
Who living, earned a world's revering thought,
  And dying, leaves his name without a stain !

DEDICATORY ADDRESS AT GETTYSBURG.

ABRAHAM LINCOLN.

FOURSCORE and seven years ago, our fathers brought forth upon this continent a new nation, conceived in liberty, and dedicated to the proposition that all men are created equal. Now we are engaged in a great civil war, testing whether that nation—or any nation, so conceived and so dedicated—can long endure. We are met on a great battle-field of that war. We are met to dedicate a portion of it as the final resting-place of those who have given their lives that that nation might live. It is altogether fitting and proper that we should do this. But, in a larger sense, we cannot dedicate, we cannot consecrate, we cannot hallow, this ground. The brave men, living and dead, who struggled here, have consecrated it, far above our power to add or to detract. The world will very little note, nor long remember what we say here ; but it can never forget what they did here. It is for us, the living, rather to be dedicated, here, to the unfinished work that they have thus far so nobly carried on. It is rather for us to be here dedicated to the great task remaining before us; that from these honored dead we take increased devotion to that cause for which they here gave the last full measure of devotion ; that we here highly resolve that these dead shall not have died in vain ; that the nation shall, under God, have a new birth of freedom, and that government of the people, by the people, for the people, shall not perish from the earth.

JOHN HANCOCK.

ROBERT C. WINTHROP.

WAS there ever a more signal distinction vouchsafed to mortal man than that which was won and worn by John Hancock a hundred years ago to-day? Not altogether a great man ; not without some grave defects of character ;—we remember nothing at this hour save his Presidency of the Congress of the Declaration, and the bold and noble signature to our Magna Charta.

Behold him in the chair which is still standing in its old place,—the very same chair in which Washington was to sit eleven years later as President of the Convention which framed the Constitution of the United States ; the very same chair, emblazoned on the back of which Franklin was to descry "a rising, and not a setting sun," when that Constitution had been finally adopted,—behold him, the young Boston merchant, not yet quite forty years of age, not only with a princely fortune at stake, but with a price at that moment upon his own head, sitting there to-day in all the calm composure and dignity which so peculiarly characterized him, and which nothing seemed able to relax or ruffle.

Behold him ! He has risen for a moment. He has put the question. The Declaration is adopted. It is already late in the evening, and all formal promulgation of the day's doings must be postponed. After a grace of three days, the air will be vibrating with the joyous tones of the Old Bell in the cupola over his head, proclaiming Liberty to all mankind, and with the responding acclamations of assembled multitudes. Meantime, for him, however, a simple but solemn duty remains to be discharged. The paper is before him. You may see the very table on which it was laid, and the very inkstand which awaits his use. No hesitation now. He dips his pen, and with an untrembling hand proceeds to execute a signature, which would seem to have been studied in the schools, and practiced in the counting-room, and shaped and modeled day by day in the correspondence of mercantile and political manhood, until it should be meet for the authentication of some immortal act ; and which, as Webster grandly said, has made his name as imperishable " as if it were written between Orion and the Pleiades."

Under that signature, with only the attestation of a secretary, the Declaration goes forth to the American people, to be printed in their journals, to be proclaimed in their streets, to be published from their pulpits, to be read at the head of their armies, to be incorporated forever into their history. The British forces, driven away from Boston, are now landing on Staten Island, and the reverses of Long Island are just awaiting us. They were met by the promulgation of this act of offense and defiance to all loyal authority. But there was no individual responsibility for that act, save the signature of John Hancock, President, and Charles Thomson, Secretary.

Not until the 2d of August was our young Boston merchant relieved from the perilous, the appalling grandeur of standing sole sponsor for the revolt of Thirteen Colonies and Three Millions of people. Sixteen or seventeen years before, as a very young man, he had made a visit to London, and was present at the burial of George II. and at the coronation of George III. He is now not only the witness but the instrument, and in some sort the impersonation, of a far more substantial change of dynasty on his own soil—the burial of royalty under any and every title, and the coronation of a Sovereign whose scepter has already endured for a century, and whose sway has already embraced three times thirteen States and more than thirteen times three millions of people !—*From Oration at Boston, 4th July, 1876.*

—————

JOHN ADAMS.

ROBERT C. WINTHROP.

ONE more name is still to be pronounced. One more star of that little Massachusetts cluster is still to be observed and noted. And it is one which, on the precise occasion we commemorate,—one which, during those great days of June and July, 1776, on which the question of Independence was immediately discussed and decided,—had hardly "a fellow in the firmament," and which was certainly " the bright, particular star " of our own constellation. You will all have anticipated me in naming John Adams. Beyond all doubt his is the Massachusetts name most prominently associated with the immediate Day we celebrate.

Others may have been earlier or more active than he in preparing the way. Others may have labored longer and more zealously to instruct the popular mind and inflame the popular heart for the great step which was now to be taken. Others may have been more ardent, as they unquestionably were more prominent, in the various stages of the struggle against Writs of Assistance, and Stamp Acts, and Tea Taxes. But from the date of that marvelous letter of his to Nathan Webb, in 1755, when he was less than twenty years old, he seems to have forecast the destinies of this continent as few other men of any age at that day had done ; while from the moment at which the Continental Congress took the question of Independence fairly in hand, as a question to be decided and acted on, until they had brought it to its final issue in the Declaration, his was the voice, above and before all other voices, which commanded the ears, convinced the minds, and inspired the hearts of his colleagues, and triumphantly secured the result.

I need not speak of him in other relations or in after years. His long life of varied and noble service to his country, in almost every sphere of public duty, domestic and foreign, belongs to history ; and history has long ago taken it in charge. But the testimony which was borne to his grand efforts and utterances, by the author of the Declaration himself, can never be gainsaid, never be weakened, never be forgotten. That testimony, old as it is, familiar as it is, belongs to this day. John Adams will be remembered and honored forever, in every true American heart, as the acknowledged Champion of Independence in the Continental Congress, " coming out with a power which moved us from our seats,"—" our Colossus on the floor."

And when we recall the circumstances of his death,—the year, the day, the hour,—and the last words upon his dying lips, "Independence forever,"—who can help feeling that there was some mysterious tie holding back his heroic spirit from the skies, until it should be set free amid the exulting shouts of his country's first National Jubilee !—*July 4th, 1876.*

JEFFERSON AND ADAMS.

ROBERT C. WINTHROP.

In my rapid survey of the men assembled at Philadelphia a hundred years ago to-day, I began with Thomas Jefferson of Virginia, and I end with John Adams of Massachusetts, and no one can hesitate to admit that, under God, they were the very alpha and omega of that day's doings—the pen and the tongue—the masterly author, and the no less masterly advocate, of the Declaration.

And now, my friends, what legend of ancient Rome or Greece or Egypt, what myth of prehistoric mythology, what story of Herodotus, or fable of Æsop, or metamorphosis of Ovid, would have seemed more fabulous and mythical—did it rest on any remote or doubtful tradition, or had not so many of us lived to be startled and thrilled and awed by it—than the fact, that these two men, under so many different circumstances and surroundings, of age and constitution and climate widely distant from each other, living alike in quiet neighborhoods, remote from the smoke and stir of cities, and long before railroads and telegraphs had made any advances toward the annihilation or abridgment of space, should have been released to their rest and summoned to the skies, not only on the same day, but that day the Fourth of July, and that Fourth of July the Fiftieth Anniversary of that great Declaration which they had contended for and carried through so triumphantly side by side !

And now another Fifty Years have passed away, and we are holding our high Centennial Festival ; and still that most striking, most impressive, most memorable coincidence in all American history, or even in the authentic records of man-kind, is without a visible monument anywhere !

In the interesting little city of Weimar, renowned as the resort and residence of more than one of the greatest philos-ophers and poets of Germany, many a traveler must have seen and admired the charming statues of Goethe and Schiller, standing side by side and hand in hand, on a single pedestal, and offering, as it were, the laurel wreath of literary priority or pre-eminence to each other. Few nobler works of art, in conception or execution, can be found on the Continent of Europe.

And what could be a worthier or a juster commemoration of the marvelous coincidence of which I have just spoken, and of the men who are the subjects of it, and of the Declara-tion with which, alike in their lives and in their deaths, they are so peculiarly and so signally associated, than just such a Monument, with the statues of Adams and Jefferson, side by side and hand in hand, upon the same base, pressing upon each other, in mutual acknowledgment and deference, the victor palm of triumph for which they must ever be held in common and equal honor ! It would be a new tie between Massachusetts and Virginia. It would be a new bond of that Union which is the safety and glory of both. It would be a new pledge of that restored good-will between the North and South, which is the herald and harbinger of a Second Century of National Independence. It would be a fit recognition of the great Hand of God in our history !

Before all other statues, let us have those of Adams and Jefferson on a single block, as they stood together a hundred years ago to-day—as they were translated together just fifty years ago to-day :—foremost for Independence in their lives, and in their deaths not divided !—*July 4th, 1876.*

FREEDOM.

MRS. HELEN HUNT.

WHAT freeman knoweth freedom ? Never he
  Whose fathers' fathers through long lines have reigned
  O'er kingdoms which mere heritage hath gained.
Though from his youth to age he roam as free
As winds, he dreams not freedom's ecstasy.
  But he whose birth was in a nation chained
  For centuries ; whose very breath was drained
From breasts of slaves that knew not there could be
  Such thing as freedom ; he knows when its light
  Bursts, dazzling ; though the glory blind his sight.
He knows the joy. Fools sneer because he reels,
  And wields confusedly his infant will.
The wise man, watching, with a heart that feels,
  Says : " Cure for freedom's harms is freedom still."

———•———

CALDWELL OF SPRINGFIELD.

BRET HARTE.

HERE'S the spot. Look around you. Above, on the height,
Lay the Hessians, encamped. By that church on the right
Stood the gaunt Jersey farmers. And here ran a wall—
You may dig anywhere and you'll turn up a ball.
Nothing more. Grasses spring, waters run, flowers blow,
Pretty much as they did ninety-three years ago.

Nothing more, did I say ? Stay one moment ; you've heard
Of Caldwell, the pastor, who once preached the Word
Down at Springfield ? What ! no ? Come—that's bad ; why
      he had
All the Jerseys aflame ! And they gave him the name
Of the " Rebel high priest. " He stuck in their gorge,
For he loved the Lord God, and he hated King George !

He had cause, you might say ! When the Hessians, that day,
Marched up with Knyphausen, they stopped on their way
At the " Farms," where his wife, with a child in her arms,
Sat alone in the house. How it happened none knew
But God, and that one of the hireling crew
Who fired the shot. Enough ! there she lay,
And Caldwell, the chaplain, her husband, away !

Did he preach—did he pray ? Think of him, as you stand
By the old church, to-day ; think of him and that band
Of militant plowboys ! See the smoke and the heat
Of that reckless advance—of that straggling retreat !
Keep the ghost of that wife, foully slain, in your view,
And what could you, what would you, what should you do ?

Why just what he did ! They were left in the lurch
For the want of more wadding. He ran to the church,
Broke the door, stripped the pews, and dashed out in the road
With his arms full of hymn-books, and threw down his load
At their feet ! Then, above all the shouting and shots,
Rang his voice—" Put Watts into 'em, boys ! give 'em
　　　Watts ! "

And they did ! That is all. Grasses spring, flowers blow
Pretty much as they did ninety-three years ago.
You may dig anywhere, and you'll turn up a ball,
But not always a hero like this—and that's all.

BOSTON BOYS.—(GRANDFATHER'S STORY.)

NORA PERRY.

WHAT ! you want to hear a story all about that old-time glory,
　　When your grandsires fought for freedom against the
　　　　British crown ;
When King George's redcoats mustered all their forces, to
　　　　be flustered
　　By our Yankee raw recruits, from each village and each
　　　　town ;

And the very boys protested, when they thought their
 rights molested?
My father used to tell us how the British General
 stared
With a curious, dazed expression when the youngsters in
 procession
Filed before him in a column, not a whit put out
 or scared.

Then the leader told his story,—told the haughty, handsome
 Tory
 How his troops there, on the mall there (what you call
  " the common," dears),
All the winter through had vexed them, meddled with them
 and perplexed them,
 Flinging back to their remonstrance only laughter,
  threats, and sneers.

" What ! " the General cried in wonder,—and his tones
 were tones of thunder,—
 " Are these the rebel lessons that your fathers taught
  you, pray?
Did they send such lads as you here, to make such bold
 ado here,
 And flout King George's officers upon the King's
  highway ? "

Up the little leader started, while heat lightning flashed
 and darted
 From his blue eyes, as he answered, stout of voice, with
  all his might:
" No one taught us, let me say, sir ; no one sent us here
 to-day, sir ;
 But we're Yankees, Yankees, Yankees, and the Yankees
  know their rights !

" And your soldiers at the first, sir, on the mall there, did
   their worst, sir;
 Pulled our snow-hills down we'd built there, broke the
   ice upon the pond ;
' Help it, help it if you can, then !' back they answered
   every man, then,
 When we asked them, sir, to quit it; and we said, ' This
   goes beyond

' " ' Soldiers' rights or soldiers' orders, for we've kept within
   our borders
 To the south'ard of the mall there, where we've always
   had our play ! ' "
" Where you always shall hereafter, undisturbed by threats
   or laughter
 From my officers or soldiers. Go, my brave boys ! from
   · this day

" Troops of mine shall never harm you, never trouble or
   alarm you,"
 Suddenly ·the British General, moved with admiration,
   cried.
In a minute caps were swinging, five and twenty voices
   ringing
 In a shout and cheer that summoned every neighbor, far
   and wide.

And these neighbors told the story how the haughty,
   handsome Tory,
 Bowing, smiling, hat in hand there, faced the little rebel
   band ;
How he said, just then and after, half in earnest, half in
   laughter :
 " So it seems the very children strike for freedom in
   this land ! "

So I tell you now the story all about that old-time
     glory,
As my father's father told it long and long ago to
     me ;
How they met and had it out there, what he called their
     bloodless bout there ;
How he felt——" What ! was he there, then ? "   Why,
     the *leader*, that was he !

GREAT MEN.

ROBERT C. WINTHROP.

WHO, and what, are great men ?   " And now stand forth,"
says an eminent Swiss historian, who had completed a survey
of the whole history of mankind, at the very moment when, as
he says, " a blaze of freedom is just bursting forth beyond the
ocean,"—" And now stand forth, ye gigantic forms, shades of
the first Chieftains, and Sons of Gods, who glimmer among
the rocky halls and mountain fortresses of the ancient world ;
and you Conquerors of the world from Babylon and Mace-
donia ; ye Dynasties of Cæsars, of Huns, Arabs, Moguls, and
Tartars ; ye Commanders of the Faithful on the Tigris, and
Commanders of the Faithful on the Tiber ; you hoary Counsel-
lors of Kings, and Peers of Sovereigns ; Warriors on the car
of triumph, covered with scars, and crowned with laurels ; ye
long rows of Consuls and Dictators, famed for your lofty minds,
your unshaken constancy, your ungovernable spirit ;—stand
forth, and let us survey for awhile your assembly, like a Coun-
cil of the Gods ! What were ye ? The first among mortals ?
Seldom can you claim that title ! The best of men ? Still fewer
of you have deserved such praise ! Were ye the compellers,
the instigators of the human race, the prime movers of all
their works ? Rather let us say that you were the instruments,
that you were the wheels, by whose means the Invisible Being
has conducted the incomprehensible fabric of universal government across the ocean of time ! "

Instruments and wheels of the Invisible Governor of the Universe ! This is indeed all which the greatest of men ever have been or ever can be. No flatteries of courtiers ; no adulations of the multitude ; no audacity of self-reliance ; no intoxications of success ; no evolutions or developments of science, can make more or other of them. This is "the seamark of their utmost sail," the goal of their farthest run, the very round and top of their highest soaring.

Oh, if there could be, to-day, a deeper and more pervading impression of this great truth throughout our land, and a more prevailing conformity of our thoughts and words and acts to the lessons which it involves ; if we could lift ourselves to a loftier sense of our relations to the Invisible ; if, in surveying our past history, we could catch larger and more exalted views of our destinies and our responsibilities ; if we could realize that the want of good men may be a heavier woe to a land than any want of what the world calls great men, our Centennial Year would not only be signalized by splendid ceremonials and magnificent commemorations and gorgeous expositions ; but it would go far toward fulfilling something of the grandeur of that "Acceptable Year" which was announced by higher than human lips, and would be the auspicious promise and pledge of a glorious second century of Independence and Freedom for our country !

For, if that second century of self-government is to go on safely to its close, or is to go on safely and prosperously at all, there must be some renewal of that old spirit of subordination and obedience to Divine, as well as human Laws, which has been our security in the past. There must be faith in something higher and better than ourselves. There must be a reverent acknowledgment of an Unseen but All-seeing, All-controlling Ruler of the Universe. His Word, His Day, His House, His Worship, must be sacred to our children, as they have been to their fathers ; and His blessing must never fail to be invoked upon our land and upon our liberties. The patriot voice, which cried from the balcony of yonder Old State House, when the Declaration had been originally proclaimed, "Stability and Perpetuity to American Independence," did not fail to add, "God save our American States." I would prolong that ancestral prayer. And the last phrase to pass my lips at this hour, and to take its chance of remembrance or oblivion in years to come, as the conclusion of this Centennial oration, and the sum of all I can say to the present or the future, shall be :—There is, there can be, no independence of God : in Him, as a Nation, no less than in Him, as individuals, "we live and move, and have our being !" GOD SAVE OUR AMERICAN STATES !—*July 4th, 1876.*

EULOGY OF STONEWALL JACKSON.

GOV. KEMPER, OF VIRGINA.

WITH a mother's tears and love, with ceremonies to be chronicled in her archives and transmitted to the latest posterity, the Commonwealth this day emblazons the virtues, and consecrates in enduring bronze the image, of her mighty dead. In every country, and for all mankind, Stonewall Jackson's career of unconscious heroism will go down as an inspiration, teaching the power of courage and conscience and faith directed to the glory of God. It speaks to our fellow-citizens of the North, and reviving no animosities of the bloody past, it commands their respect for the valor, the manhood, the integrity and honor of the people of whom this Christian warrior was a representative type and champion. It speaks to our stricken brethren of the South, bringing back his sublime simplicity and faith, his knightly and incorruptible fidelity to each engagement of duty ; and it stands an enduring admonition and guaranty that sooner shall the sun reverse its course in the heavens than his comrades and his compatriot people shall prove recreant to the parole and contract of honor which binds them, in the fealty of freemen, to the Constitution and Union of these States. It speaks with equal voice to every portion of the reunited common country, warning all that impartial justice and impartial right, to the

North and to the South, are the only pillars on which the arch of the Federal Union can securely rest. It represents the unbought spirit of honor, and stands forth before the world a mute protest against the rule of tyrants.

Let the spirit and design with which we erect this memorial to-day admonish our whole country that the actual reconciliation of the States must come, and so far as honorably in us lies, shall come ; but that its work will never be complete until the equal honor and equal liberties of each section shall be acknowledged, vindicated, and maintained by both. We have buried the strifes and passions of the past ; we now perpetuate impartial honor to whom honor is due, and, stooping to resent no criticism, we stand with composure and trust ready to greet every token of just and constitutional pacification. Let this statue stand, with its mute eloquence, to inspire our children with patriotic fervor and to maintain the prolific power of the Commonwealth in bringing forth men as of old. Let Virginia, beholding her past in the light of this event, take heart and rejoice in her future. Mother of States and sages and heroes ! bowed in sorrow, with bosom bruised and wounded, with garments rent and rolled in blood, arise and dash away all tears ! No stain dims your glittering escutcheon ! Let your brow be lifted up with the glad consciousness of unbroken pride and unsullied honor ! Demand and resume complete possession of your ancient place in the sisterhood of States ; and go forward to the great destiny which, in virtue of the older and the later days, belongs to the co-sovereign Commonwealth of Virginia.—*From address at the unvailing of Jackson's Statue, at Richmond, Oct. 26, 1875.*

A CENTENNIAL ODE.

BY A CONFEDERATE OFFICER.

YE soldiers of America,
  In civil warfare proved,
Whether you gained what valor sought
  Or lost the cause you loved ;

Come forth again, and close around
  The ancient standard throng,
And strong let your song
  O'er the storm of faction rise :
" The Blue and Gray against the world
  For all that freemen prize ! "

The spirits of your fallen
  Shall start from every mound
Where they lie cold, and lift the strain
  From consecrated ground.
Where Hill and gallant Wadsworth sleep
  Shall swell the mighty sound,
As strong peals your song,
  And echoes to the skies :
" No slavery for North or South
  Till every soldier dies ! "

Our freedom has no champions
  So loyal to the core
As these who 'mid the thunderous guns
  Their harness bravely wore ;
They loved the sacred boon of peace,
  Whatever flag they bore ;
And their cheer rises clear,
  As they march to save the land,
With starry flag o'er Blue and Gray,
  All brothers hand in hand !

The day-star of our country
  Shall yet triumphant shine ;
They will not stoop to nurture wrath
  Whose blood has poured like wine.
Then peace shall hail you warriors,
  And crown your work divine ;
And your name all aflame
  With bloodless glory won,
Shall live till History's voice is mute,
  And Freedom's life is done.

"MISSING."

GENERAL M'MAHON.

IN the beginning of your solemn pilgrimage to the graves of the unforgotten dead, it is fitting, comrades, that for a moment you should halt reverently here in the very heart of the great city that is the heart of the nation, to pay your tribute of flowers to him who was the nation's great defender. Commander of its armies and its fleets, director of its destinies in the days of its supremest peril, intrusted with powers never before given to an American citizen, it is enough to say of him in eulogy to-day, in the simple words of the Roman, " He has deserved well of the Republic." This is the language of the flowers with which you have crowned him ; yet there is another significance, tender and more touching, which, with your permission, I will attach to your simple ceremonies here. They mean more than a mere tribute to the memory of the illustrious President. There are thousands of our departed comrades whose remains have never been gathered into those great cities of the dead, which to-day are visited and made beautiful by your votive offerings. They sleep in distant church-yards, remote from the pious care of comrades. They rest in unmarked and uncoffined graves, where they were hastily laid beneath the trampled fields on which they died. They lie beneath the waters of swift rivers in the West. With "heavy-shotted hammock shroud," from the decks of stately battle-ships at sea, they were reverently intrusted to the " vast and wandering grave " of the deep. Amid the corals of the Gulf they rest beneath shattered decks or entombed between the iron bulkheads which had been their home upon the waters. Their ashes were scattered by the winds of heaven in those terrible days in the Wilderness, when the consuming flames, fiercer than the wrath of man, sparing neither our wounded nor our dead, swept through the tangled forest by night after the tide of battle had drifted onward toward the end. For none of these shall the gentle hands of kin or comrade to-day lay sweet flowers upon their resting-places. Their sole epitaph is that word of deepest pathos in the battle record, " Missing." They went to the field and they came not back ; where they fell, or how, a mystery forever here, but not unmarked of Him who notes even a sparrow's fall. With each recurring year let it be known that on this spot, and at this hour, in the name of Abraham Lincoln, we honor with our floral offerings the memory of all our dead, wherever they may rest, whose graves cannot be visited. No higher honor could be paid to him, no sweeter tribute could be rendered unto them.

DECORATION DAY.

MAY 30, 1876.

" FORWARD ! " was the word when day
Dawned upon the armed array.

" Fallen ! " was the word when night
Closed upon the field of fight.

" Wounded ? " " Yes ! " " Where ? " " In the breast ! "
Bear him back, then, with the rest.

Only one of many more !
When, oh, when will war be o'er ! ·

" Hurt, my boy ? " " Oh, no, not much !
Only got a little touch."

" Wonder what the folks would say
If they knew the news to-day."

" Forward ! " was the word that flashed
Homeward when the cannon crashed.

" What's the news ? " When night had come,
" Missing ! " was the word sent home.

"Fallen ?"   "Yes. He fell, they say,
In the fiercest of the fray !"

"Died last night !" the message said.
So the morrow's papers read.

Not a murmur, not a sigh—
Oh ! 'tis glory thus to die !

How her heart heaves ! Bows her head !
"Mother, mother !" Mother's dead !

———

Two green graves we'll deck to-day,
    Son's and mother's side by side ;
None will dare to tell us, Nay !
    Both for Right and Freedom died.

While we honor him who fell
    In the fiercest of the fray,
We will honor her as well
    Lying by his side to-day.

Let the flowers forever fair
    Bloom above the sleeping braves ;
While the angels guard them there,
    Glory lingers round their graves.
                    —*N. Y. Evening Post.*

———

A NAMELESS GRAVE.

HENRY WADSWORTH LONGFELLOW.

"A SOLDIER of the Union mustered out,"
    Is the inscription on an unknown grave
    At Newport News, beside the salt sea-wave,
Nameless and dateless, sentinel or scout,
Shot down in skirmish or disastrous rout
    Of battle, when the loud artillery drave
    Its iron wedges through the ranks of brave
And doomed battalions storming the redoubt !

Thou unknown hero, sleeping by the sea
In thy forgotten grave ! with secret shame
I feel my pulses beat, my forehead burn,
When I remember thou hast given fame,
All that thou hadst, thy life, thy very name,
And I can give thee nothing in return.

A WAYSIDE GRAVE.

MARY R. D. DINGWALL.

A LITTLE mound, a narrow, nameless bed
Where sleeps a Union soldier mustered in
To that fair land beyond the battle's din.
Amazed that I so long forgot, I sped
To place my floral gift above the head
Of him who gave his name and life to win
Freedom and peace to our rent land again ;
But faithful Nature, there before me, shed
Fragrance of violet and wild-rose spray ;
A weeping birch its tender branches spread,
While wind, sun, rain, and birds, and pregnant May
In perfume, flower, and song, and promise said,
"Christ knows his dead, and in the judgment day
Will call *his name* who sleeps beside the way."

THE TRUE FRIENDS OF THE UNION.

STEWART L. WOODFORD.

AMONG these graves we would not recall one memory of
bitterness and anger. With equal love for what was good
in their common humanity, with equal forgiveness for what
was evil, Nature folds alike the ashes of loyalist and rebel in
her resurrection robes of spring-time flowers. Courage and
honor alike require that we, who by God's providence were
victors in the strife, should be freely and absolutely generous
in peace. Courage and honor equally require that they who
were beaten should yield manly submission to the decision of
that final tribunal of the sword to which they appealed.

3*

Does any seek this day, for any cause, to revive the old prejudice of class and caste and race ? He is no friend of the Union. Does any seek this day, for self or partisan success, to set white against black or black against white ? He is no friend of the Union. The man who this day draws the color line in politics is either traitor, knave, or simpleton. His place is among the shadows and bats of the past, and not in the sunlight of the present. Does any seek to deny to loyal comers in any part of the South full citizenship, complete protection, and hearty welcome, because such comers wore the Federal blue in other days ? He is no friend of the Union. Does any seek to taunt loyal subjects of the law and keepers of the peace, because such wore the gray in days of battle ? He is no friend of the Union.

Where so-called Conservatism has triumphed at the South there have been too often practical intolerance, practical denial of personal liberty, practical denial of popular education, and persistent effort to revive old systems under new forms. Where so-called Radicalism has succeeded there have been too often official corruption and venality. One turns in sadness from such partisanship on either side and asks for a patriotism of conscience, courage, and common sense, that will neither coerce the ballot of the citizen nor steal the revenue of the State ; that will deal with white and black alike in the great but rare wisdom of simple justice ; that will seek to perform each public trust with brave fidelity and intelligent honesty.

Not upon others only, but equally upon ourselves, this hour lays its injunction. Let no man feel, as he turns from this memorial meeting and goes back to his daily living, that he can safely or justly neglect the personal performance of his individual political duty.

Any failure to have good government under our system is as much our fault as that of our rulers. Nay, it is mainly our fault, for with us lies the final power. When we deliberately resolve, they must either execute our purpose or give place to such as will.

This is the lesson I would press home this day upon each brain and conscience,—the personal performance by each citizen of his individual duty to the State.—*Decoration Day, 1876.*

THE PATRIOTS AND HEROES OF 1861.

M. H. BUCKHAM.

NEVER has history witnessed a more splendid uprising of a great people to its heaven-appointed mission ; not when Greece resisted the Persian, nor Rome the Carthaginian, nor Switzerland the Burgundian, nor England the Spaniard, nor Spain the Frenchman, nor America herself her unnatural parent in the days of Revolutionary glory. And when we say the nation did this, we mean that the men who sleep here under this sod, and the thousands who sleep elsewhere, they did it. When the hour came which put the question to the test, whether the nation had lost its virtue and heroism, its conscience and faith, these men came forth and refuted the slander. The world had almost forgotten that America had ever had any other history than that connected with her material progress and her peculiar institution. We had come to be regarded as a nation of money-getters and braggarts, utterly destitute of the stuff out of which great men are made. Europe had long been waiting for the crisis which was to demonstrate the feebleness and instability of the character brought out of such political institutions as ours. But the crisis did come, and reverses came, reverses such as most severely try the mettle of a people.

And when foreign statesmen saw to their amazement that reverses served but to awaken the national spirit, that tidings of disaster were the best means of filling the army and the treasury ; when at length from all sections of the country came the demand upon the Government : " Count upon us for any number of men and any amount of money, for our courage is now up and there is nothing that we cannot and will not do to save the country ; " when these statesmen saw that the

Americans of to-day, like their ancestors of old, were capable of giving and doing and suffering everything for an idea, they were obliged to confess, as one of them did in Parliament, "These men have taught us a new respect for the human race." Accordingly, when a second crisis came, and England and America stood front to front, ready for peace or war at the turning of the scale, the proudest nation in Europe honored herself in the judgment of the world by respecting the equal dignity of the American Republic. And this, also, these men accomplished for us.

And, last and greatest boon of all, by their sacrifices and sufferings, by their toil and their blood, they have given us a past atoned for, and a future untrammeled. After such a history as this nation enacted from 1830 to 1860, it was written in the unalterable laws of Providential justice that there was no future for the nation unless that past of wrong and crime was washed out by rivers of penitential tears and seas of expiatory blood. That heavy debt of retributive justice, let us trust, has been paid fully, as it certainly was paid freely. A great chasm divides the America of 1873 from the America of 1860. Into that chasm these men plunged themselves with more than Roman heroism, in order that we might reach the firm highway of national safety and progress. Upon that highway the nation has now entered. With secure and elastic step it is now urging its ascent up the path of greatness to a height not yet attained by any people, and not even dreamed of in the Utopias of the sages. But if we forget those whose agony and blood paid the penalty of our national crime, whose strong faith in God and the righteous cause wrought out our deliverance and achieved. for us our possible future, then be assured that the curse of God will descend upon a people guilty of such ingratitude, and history will justify the avenging wrath under which they fell.—*Decoration Day, 1873.*

ONE IN BLUE AND ONE IN GRAY.

EACH thin hand resting on a grave,
　Her lips apart in prayer,
A mother knelt and left her tears
　Upon the violets there.
O'er many a rood of vale and lawn,
　Of hill and forest gloom,
The reaper Death had reveled in
　His fearful harvest-home.
The last red Summer's sun had shone
　Upon a fruitless fray;
From yonder forest charged the blue,
　Down yonder slope the gray.

The hush of death was on the scene ;
　And sunset o'er the dead,
In that oppressive stillness,
　A pall of glory spread.
I know not, dare not question how
　I met the ghastly glare
Of each upturned and stirless face
　That shrunk and whitened there.
I knew my noble boys had stood
　Through all that withering day ;
I knew that Willie wore the blue,
　That Harry wore the gray.

I thought of Willie's clear blue eye,
　His wavy hair of gold,
That clustered on a fearless brow
　Of purest Saxon mold ;
Of Harry, with his raven locks,
　And eagle glance of pride :
Of how they clasped each other's han
　And left their mother's side ;

How hand in hand they bore my prayers
   And blessings on the way,—
A noble heart beneath the blue,
   Another 'neath the gray.

The dead, with white and folded hands,
   That hushed our village homes,
I've seen laid calmly, tenderly,
   Within their darkened rooms ;
But *there* I saw distorted limbs,
   And many an eye aglare,
In the soft purple twilight of
   The thunder-smitten air ;
Along the slope and on the sward
   In ghastly ranks they lay,
And there was blood upon the blue,
   And blood upon the gray.

I looked and saw his blood, and his :
   A swift and vivid dream
Of blended years flashed o'er me, when
   Like some cold shadow, came
A blindness of the eye and brain—
   The same that seizes one
When men are smitten suddenly
   Who overstare the sun ;
And while, blurred with the sudden stroke
   That swept my soul, I lay,—
They buried Willie in his blue,
   And Harry in his gray.

The shadows fall upon their graves ;
   They fall upon my heart ;
And through the twilight of my soul
   Like dew the tears will start.

The starlight comes so silently,
   And lingers where they rest ;
So hope's revealing starlight sinks
   And shines within my breast.
They ask not there, where yonder heaven
   Smiles with eternal day,
Why Willie wore the loyal blue—
Why Harry wore the gray.

ADDRESS OF WELCOME TO THE WASHINGTON LIGHT INFANTRY, OF SOUTH CAROLINA.

JOSIAH QUINCY.

IN behalf of the citizzns of Boston, in behalf of the inhabitants of Massachusetts, and as representative of the whole people of the North, citizens of South Carolina, I cordially welcome you to the historic scenes of another century. A hundred years ago the sons of Boston, inspired with the spirit and aided by the arms of the citizens and yeomanry of the adjoining country, commenced a struggle that terminated in American Independence. Their numbers were few, scarce exceeding the inhabitants of a single ward in this city, when they threw down the gauntlet to the mightiest naval power in the world.

The thirteen stripes on yonder banner remind us of the number of small States scattered along the borders of the ocean, or clinging to the banks of a few rivers, that constituted the colonies. But they were all alive to the importance of securing and maintaining the liberties of Englishmen. From the Highlands of the Hudson and the Green Mountains of Vermont, from the high hills of the Santee and the crests of the Alleghanies, came resolute men, whose blood was shed that the spirit of freedom might clothe itself in a nobler shape than the world had yet seen.

It was the vital issue of that time that all forms of privileged right must give way before the natural rights of man, to freedom of thought, and freedom of religion, and that no exercise of power could be tolerated that did not carry with it the co-operation of an enlightened public opinion.   It was for this—whether distinctly recognized or not—it was for this that the shots were fired a hundred years ago on Bunker's Hill.   It was to establish the republican principle in this new world—to root it firmly in our virgin soil.   We will not here remember any difficulties and misunderstandings that have been encountered on our way toward the full development of this republican principle.   They have been bravely met by brave men from the representative States of South Carolina and Massachusetts, who to-day join hands and thank God that, while he has educated and proved us by temporary evils, he has spared us from the permanent evil inseparable from any form of monarchy.

Fifty years ago, as aid to the Governor of Massachusetts, I received the veterans who took part in the battle you have come to commemorate.   Fifty years ago I stood beside the great Massachusetts statesman, when he spoke to the nation from Bunker's Hill.   Would that I could recall the tones in which he called us to forget all sectional feeling, and devote ourselves to our country, our whole country, and nothing but our country.   He is no longer here to invigorate our minds with his mighty conceptions or to magnetize us with his eloquence.   But in his familiar language, let us renew our allegiance to that central sovereignty which is our hope and the hope of the world.   Soldiers and citizens of South Carolina, of New York and Massachusetts, of North and South, of East and West, let us here clasp hands and repeat together the words that shall echo on, when we and our children shall cease to be : " LIBERTY AND UNION, NOW AND FOREVER, ONE AND INSEPARABLE !"—*The day before the 100th Anniversary of the Battle of Bunker's Hill, June 16th, 1875.*

RESPONSE TO THE FOREGOING ADDRESS OF WELCOME.

LIEUTENANT SIMONS, OF THE WASHINGTON LIGHT INFANTRY.

MR. CHAIRMAN, Fellow Soldiers, and Fellow Citizens of Boston : Bad, indeed, must be that heart which cannot draw inspiration of patriotism from a scene like the present. We are strangers and aliens no longer, but brethren and fellow citizens of one common country.

Our fathers stood together when they for the first time gave to the world a government of true liberty, and in that day when in these hallowed streets the sons of Massachusetts, with sturdy independence and noble spirit, determined first to be free, they found an answering echo from the shores of the State of Carolina, that said to them, We will stand by you. There was no section of the country which gave a more cordial sympathy or warmer support to the cause of American independence.

And, sir, when to-morrow we shall view that sacred spot where our fathers shed their blood for that holy cause of independence, we will not forget what they regarded as essential to that cause so dear to the taste of the oppressed of every nation and of every clime, that in their view the very first element of success was, that the colonies should be united, not in name only, but in heart and in hope.

The late sad war is over ; the conflict has ceased. The command you see before you left one hundred and thirteen of their comrades upon the battle-field for that State whose call they regarded it their duty to follow. But they realize that, that war over, their high mission is reconciliation, peace, and fraternity. There is no higher duty which patriotism can require or invoke than that we should now meet as friends and brethren, and uphold to the remotest posterity that liberty for which our fathers shed their precious blood.

I trust it will echo and re-echo from mountain to seashore, from the lakes to the gulf, and in every city and village and hamlet and plain in this land, that South Carolina, to-day,

henceforth, and forever, will be one and inseparable for the
perpetuity of the Government and liberty under the Constitution. You have well said, Mr. Adams, springing as you do
from those who have made the name of this country illustrious,
that we desire no hollow truce ; we desire no mere profusion
of words. We want to be one in heart, in name, and in hope,
and to regard him as the enemy of his country who shall
ever attempt to disturb that peace, reconciliation, and fraternity
which is at last the bulwark and the sole bulwark of the
country.—*Boston, June 16th, 1875.*

THE LAST CHARGE.

LEAVITT HUNT.

IN yon ravine, with teeming life,
    Two thousand lodges rise :
  The Sioux in camp, but ever rife,
The warpath watch with gun and knife,
    Well armed against surprise.

But now our comrades strike the trail.
    Hail ! small, devoted band !
Three hundred of the Seventh, hail !
Who ever knew a charge to fail
    With Custer in command ?

Dare Custer charge that savage lair
    Where duty means to die ?
Gives answer quick the trumpet's blare
That sounds his last command in air :
    " In column—charge—by company ! "

Whom summons this last bugle call
    To charge the deadly pace ?
His brothers, kinsmen, doomed to fall,
They number five, but they are all
    Akin to Custer's race.

Let fall the rein, the chargers dash.
   Like tigers in a den,
Barred in, they fall 'neath rifle crash,
But falling deal the deadly gash :
   They are but one to ten.

At eve all lay, by death enrolled,
   In ghastly bivouac.
Alone Death stalked, the story told
Of men of more than Spartan mold,
   That column of attack.

The sun sank down deep-dyed in blood,
   When lo ! a phantom shade
Of kindred spirits capped with hood
In battle line, to greet them stood—
   The deathless Light Brigade.

In low salute their colors dip,
   As Custer moves before ;
Their sabers sink in veteran grip—
One gleam illumines every tip—
   To comrades as of yore.

They wheel in rear, with pennon lance,
   An escort man for man.
Their champing chargers proudly prance,
Through arch of glory they advance,
   And Custer leads the van.
          —N. Y. Evening Post.

THE REVEILLE.

HARK ! I hear the tramp of thousands,
 And of armed men the hum ;
Lo ! a nation's hosts have gathered
 Round the quick-alarming drum,
  Saying, "Come,
  Freemen, come !
Ere your heritage be wasted," said the quick-alarming drum.

"Let me of my heart take counsel ;
 War is not of life the sum ;
Who shall stay and reap the harvest,
 When the autumn days shall come ? "
  But the drum
  Echoed, "Come !
Death shall reap the bravest harvest," said the solemn-sound-
 ing drum.

"But when won the coming battle,
 What of profit springs therefrom ?
What if conquest—subjugation—
 Even greater ills become ? "
  But the drum
  Answered, "Come !
You must do the sum to prove it," said the promptly-sounding
 drum.

"What if, 'mid the cannon's thunder,
 Whistling shell and bursting bomb,
When my brothers fall around me,
 Cold should grow my heart and numb ? "
  But the drum
  Answered, "Come !
Better that, in death united, than in life a recreant—Come ! "

Thus they answered—hoping—fearing—
Some in faith, in doubting some,
Till a trumpet voice, proclaiming,
Said, "My chosen people, come!"
Then the drum,
Lo! was dumb,
For the great heart of the nation, throbbing, answered—
"Lord, we come!"—*From the German.*

THE IDEAS AT THE BASIS OF THE DECLARA-
TION OF INDEPENDENCE.

RICHARD S. STORRS, D.D.

NOT out of books, legal researches, historical inquiry, the careful and various studies of language, came that document ; but out of repeated public debate, out of manifold personal and private discussion, out of Jefferson's clear, sympathetic observation of the feeling and thought of men, out of that exquisite personal sensibility to vague and impalpable popular impulses which was in him innately combined with artistic taste, an ideal nature, and rare power of philosophical thought. The voice of the cottage as well as the college, of the Church as well as the legislative assembly, was in the paper. It echoed the talk of the farmer in homespun, as well as the classic eloquence of Lee, or the terrible tones of Patrick Henry. It gushed at last from the pen of its writer, like the fountain from the roots of Lebanon, a brimming river when it issues from the rock ; but it was because its sources had been supplied, its fullness filled by unseen springs ; by the rivulets winding far up among the cedars, and percolating through hidden crevices in the stone ; by melting snows, whose white sparkle seemed still on the stream ; by fierce rains, with which the basins above were drenched ; by even the dews, silent and wide, which had lain in stillness all night upon the hill.

The Platonic idea of the development of the State was thus realized here : first, ethics, then politics. A public opinion,

energetic and dominant, took its place from the start as the
chief instrument of the new civilization. No dashing maneu-
vers of skillful commanders, no sudden burst of popular passion, was in the Declaration ; but the vast mystery of a supreme and imperative public life, at once diffused and intense
—behind all persons, before all plans, beneath which individual wills are exalted, at whose touch the personal mind is inspired, and under whose transcendent impulse the smallest
instrument becomes of a terrific force. That made the
Declaration ; and that makes it now, in its modest brevity,
take its place with Magna Charta and the Petition of Right, as
full as they of vital force, and destined to a parallel permanence.'

They who framed it went back, indeed, to first principles.
There was something philosophic and ideal in their scheme,
as always there is when the general mind is deeply stirred.
It was not superficial. Yet they were not undertaking to establish new theories, or to build their State upon artificial
plans and abstract speculations. They were simply evolving
out of the past what therein had been latent ; were liberating
into free exhibition and unceasing activity a vital force older
than the history of their colonization. and wide as the lands
from which they came. They had the sweep of vast impulses
behind them. The slow tendencies of centuries came to sudden consummation in their Declaration, and the force of its
impact upon the affairs and the mind of the world was not to
be measured by its contents alone, but by the relation in
which these stood to all the vehement discussion and struggle
of which it was the latest outcome.—*New York, July 4th,
1876.*

THE AMERICAN DECLARATION AND THE PROGRESS OF FREEDOM.

CHARLES FRANCIS ADAMS.

THE greatest of all the fruits of the charter of Independence
has been the proclamation of liberty to the captive through a
great part of the civilized world.

The seed that has been sown broadcast over the world fell much of it as described in the Scripture, some of it sprouting too early, as in France, and yielding none but bitter fruit ; but more, after living in the ground many years, producing results most propitious to the advancement of mankind. It would be tedious for me to go into details describing the progress of the revolution that has changed the face of civilization. The principle enunciated in our precious scroll has done its work in Great Britain and in France, and most of all in the immense expanse of the territories of the Autocrat of all the Russias, who of his own mere motion proclaimed that noble decree which liberated from serfdom at one stroke 23,000,000 of the human race. This noble act will remain forever one of the grandest steps toward the elevation of mankind ever taken by the will of a sovereign of any race in any age.

But though freely conceding the spontaneous volition of the Czar in this instance, I do not hesitate to affirm that but for the subtle essence infused into the political sentiment of the age by the great Declaration of 1776, he would never have been inspired with the lofty magnanimity essential to the completion of his work.

I come next and last to the remembrance of the fearful conflict for the maintenance of the grand principle to which we had pledged ourselves at the very outset of our national career, and out of which we have, by the blessing of the Almighty, come safe and sound. The history is so fresh in our minds that there is no need of recalling its details, neither would I do so if there were, on a day consecrated like this to the harmony of the nation. Never was the first aspect of any contention surrounded by darker clouds; yet, viewing as we must its actual issue, at no time has there ever been more reason to rejoice in the present and look forward to a still more brilliant future. Now that the agony is over, who is there that will admit that he does not rejoice at the removal of the ponderous burden which weighed down our spirits in earlier days ? The great law proclaimed at the beginning of our course has been at last fully carried out. No more apologies for inconsistency to caviling and evil-minded objectors. No more unwelcome comparisons with the superior liberality of absolute monarchs in distant regions of the earth. Thank God ! now there is not a man who treads the soil of this broad land, void of offense, who in the eye of the law does not stand on the same level with every other man. If the memorable words of Thomas Jefferson, that true Apostle of Liberty, had done only this, it would alone serve to carry him aloft, high up among the benefactors of mankind. Not America alone, but Europe and Asia, and above all Africa, nay, the great globe itself, moves in an orbit never so resplendent as now.— *July 4th, 1876.*

OUR BANNER.

DEXTER SMITH.

O'ER the high and o'er the lowly
Floats that banner bright and holy
   In the rays of freedom's sun ;
In the nation's heart imbedded,
O'er our Union newly wedded,
   One in all, and all in one.

Let the banner wave forever ;
May its lustrous stars fade never,
   Till the stars shall pale on high ;
While there's right the wrong defeating,
While there's hope in true heart beating,
   Truth and freedom shall not die.

As it floated long before us,
Be it ever floating o'er us,
   O'er our land from shore to shore ;
There are freemen yet to wave it,
Millions who would die to save it,—
   Wave it, save it evermore.

HYMN FOR THE CENTENNIAL.

SEWALL S. CUTTING, D.D.

FREE by thy might, O God!
We sound thy praise abroad,
    In grand acclaim!
Through night and storm and tears,
Through dark and bloody years,
More than all strength that cheers,
    Was thy great name.

So, ever led by thee,
Right on to liberty
    Our fathers strode!
Their children own thy hand,
And o'er our goodly land
Uncovered, reverent stand,
    To worship God!

Free in the vows we speak—
Free in the laws we make—
    Here freedom's seat!
Fair cities rise in might,
Fair fields the eye delight,
Truth free upholds the right—
    O joy complete!

Rise, sons of liberty!
Rise, maids and matrons free!
    Rise, children, rise!
Hail now the hundredth year!
Hail with resounding cheer!
Let all the nations hear
    Freedom's emprise!

Sacred the tears we shed
Over the honored dead
    Of that great time !
Shout we adown the years,
' Ye, who are freedom's heirs,
Guard ye the ark that bears
    Our hope sublime ! '

Faith, law, and liberty,
Triumphant trinity,
    By thee we stand !
Long as the rivers run,
Long as endures the sun,
Our flag and country one—
    God keep our land.

———•———

A NATION'S THANKSGIVING.

LUCIUS E. CHITTENDEN.

NEVER since the landing on Plymouth Rock has the nation kept such a holiday.   To-day we cross the line of centuries and commence another period of our national existence.   Looking backward or forward, we discover abundant reason why we should greet this morning with the roar of rejoicing cannon, and flash upon the darkness of to-night the blaze of universal illumination.   It is a high privilege to stand to-day before the people gathered in mighty audiences in a thousand places, to recall to their minds the virtues and the glory of their ancestors.   It is a grand experience, surrounded by the morning glories of that century, and standing before its open gate, to see spanning the entire horizon the bow of future promise to posterity and to humanity.   Ours is a glorious heritage indeed.   To learn how our fathers gained it for us is also to learn how we and our children can preserve it.   It was not gained without a mighty sacrifice ; it cannot be preserved without watchful care.

Let the song of thanksgiving ascend from a choir of forty million voices. Let its theme be a country stretching from Ocean to Ocean, from the dark forests of the far Northwest to the balmy airs of tropical everglades; with its mines of gold and silver and all metals, its fertility in all that sustains human life and promotes human comfort; inhabited by an intelligent and progressive people, with room enough for thrice their number. Let it give thanks for the free constitutions under which all the people live; for their wise legislatures; for their love of education; their general industry, frugality, temperance, and enterprise. Let it be said in their praise that they welcome to the protection of their flag the oppressed of every land; that no slave lives beneath its folds; that no taint of color, no accident of birth, excludes any man from the highest privileges which that flag protects; and let it proclaim the mighty fact that the Government under which we live has now been tested by the heats of a century, by foreign war and domestic rebellion, by all the accidents and all the events which have wrecked other governments, while it has only demonstrated the strength of ours, because of that still greater and more momentous fact that the strength of our Government consists in the honor, the patriotism, and the integrity of the people. If these virtues can be preserved, our nation will endure as long as earth endures, until the fountains of the great deep are broken up and the elements themselves dissolve in fervent heat. A great thanksgiving of the people of a hemisphere forty millions in number is an occasion of mighty significance, when, like ours, it demands of all the world the recognition of the principles of popular government based upon the virtue of the people. It reduces the science of political economy to a single axiom which a child can comprehend: *Preserve the virtue of the people! Preserve the virtue of the people!!* Away with all political creeds and litanies, which require philosophers to comprehend them and put them into practice.— *July 4th, 1876.*

JULY FOURTH, 1876.

J. M. WINCHELL.

A CENTURY old to-day !
    Upon our spiritual sight there steals
A vision of old age ; a specter gray
Creeps to an open grave, and trembling kneels,
    And kneeling fades away.

    Yet, 'tis not death we celebrate,
Nor yet decrepitude, nor wan decay.
The shouts with which the nation greets the Day
Are full of lusty life, and faith in Fate.
Time has not lessened but increased our might ;
No specter rises, but a giant, armed
    For peaceful fight.
These are not evening shades that dim the light ;
'Tis morning, and the risen sun has charmed
    Away the dismal night.

    What is this hundred years ?
    To us a life's full span ; the tomb
That holds three generations of our race ;
    A period from out whose womb
Have come those grand discoveries which place
A thousand years of knowledge in our hands.
    So wonderful appears
This fruitful century to-day, that stands
Completed in our presence, that it seems
Its predecessors were but hurrying dreams
Fleeing away before this hundred years.

    We boast our hundred years ;
We boast our limits, washed by either sea ;
We boast our teeming millions, and that we
    All, all are free !
    Wakening our tyrants' fears,

Our jubilations shake the world,
Which makes our holiday its own,
With flags of freedom everywhere unfurled,
Waving in every zone.

Illustrious day, all hail!
We celebrate our Nation's birth!
Our songs of joy haunt every gale
And echo o'er the earth!
And not with martial sounds alone,
Of cannon's roar and trumpet's noisy blare,
We vent our joy upon the listening air,
But build a temple to the Arts, and throne
The gods of labor and design
Within its walls. Here use and beauty meet,
And here entwine
Their locks with garlands from the poet's lay;
And while the orator, in speech divine,
Sets gems of wisdom from the antique day,
The minstrel of the future strikes his lyre
In matchless strains filled with celestial fire;
And as the echoes die,
Amidst tumultuous shout and joyful cry,
The prescient ear, intent, with rapture hears
Them sounding down another hundred years!
—The Galaxy.

———◆———

AMERICA.

1876.

EDWIN B. RUSSELL.

THOU that wouldst sit among the stars,
The stars thy crown,
The glory of the world to-day,
Freedom's renown;

What song shall fitly hymn thy praise ?
What solemn note most deeply utter thee ?
Till proud of thy great height and majesty,
Thou shalt be prouder yet in Duty's ways !

Grand is thine Empire vast,
The seas its circle glow :
Its mountain pillars all
Pierce heaven with snow.
Broad rivers, shining cities, fleets of sails,
Dark forests, flowered plains, and fertile space ;
And they who dwell in thee, as yet, a race
O'er whom no taint of time or wrong prevails.

Elate in this high hour,
The noon of splendor thine,
Thou lookest on through centuries, to see
No failure—no decline !
Centered among the nations, they shall come
To thee for peace, thou sayest, for truth, for right ;
Thou feelest now that thine is peerless might,
And the world's shrine and ark hath here its home.

But humbly wear thy coronet ;
The gems may fade,
If by proud heart, or grasping hands,
Thou art betrayed.
Gray specters of old kingdoms rise to see
If what they failed to keep thou canst retain ;
They mutter o'er their tombs, "Thou shalt be slain !"
Say, shall their fate of wreck e'er fall to thee ?

No ! for the God that made thee
Bids thee dwell
Forever blest—till hate and wrong
Are lost in hell !

Thou, gathering all men to thy sacred feet,
  Shalt teach the world from East to West,
  And make them one in love and what is best,
Till the millennial dawn thy shores shalt greet.

    This is thy stately throne,
      Thy sceptered might.
    May no dark shadow, unforeseen,
      Whelm thee in night !
May no dread enemy drink thy dear blood !
  But with each century thy strength increase,
  And all their sunsets close in endless peace ;
Their stars rise over thee for fadeless good !

    Thou, that wouldst sit among the stars,
      The stars thy crown,
      Thy light, if lit in God,
      Shall not die down.
Ride on ! and Victory be thy daily word,
  Faith, hope, and love, thy daily prayer ;
  When fallen in desolation empires are,
Thy voice, through years eternal, shall he heard !
                        —*N. Y. Tribune.*

AIMS OF THE TRUE PATRIOT.

RICHARD S. STORRS, D.D.

FROM barren soils come richest grapes, and on severe and
rocky slopes the trees are often of toughest fiber. The wines
of Rüdesheim and Johannisberg cannot be grown in the
fatness of gardens, and the cedars of Lebanon disdain the
levels of marsh and meadow. So a heroism is sometimes
native to penury which luxury enervates, and the great reso-
lution which sprang up in the blast and blossomed under in-
clement skies, may lose its shapely and steadfast strength
when the air is all of summer softness. In exuberant resources is to be the coming American peril—in a swiftly-

increasing luxury of life. The old humility, hardihood, patience, are too likely to be lost when material success again
opens, as it will, all avenues to wealth, and when its brilliant
prizes solicit, as again they will, the national spirit.

Be it ours to endeavor that that temper of the fathers which
was nobler than their work shall live in the children, and
exalt their coming career ; that political intelligence, patriotic
devotion, a reverent spirit toward Him who is above, and
exulting expectation of the future of the world, and a sense of
our relation to it, shall be, as of old, essential forces in our
public life ; that education and religion shall keep step with
the nation's advance, and be forever instantly at home where-
ever its flag shakes out its folds.

In a spirit worthy of the memories of the past let us set
ourselves to accomplish the tasks which in the sphere of
national politics still await completion. We burn the sunshine of other years when we ignite the wood or coal upon
our hearths. We enter a privilege which ages have secured
in our daily enjoyment of political freedom. While the kind-
ling glow irradiates our homes, let it shed its luster on our
spirit and quicken it for its further work. Let us fight against
the tendency of educated men to reserve themselves from
politics, remembering that no other form of activity is so
grand or effective as that which affects, first the character, and
then the revelation of character in the government of a great
and free people. Let us make religious dissensions here, as
a force in politics, as absurd as witchcraft. Let party names
be nothing to us, in comparison with that costly and proud in-
heritance of liberty and of law which parties exist to conserve
and enlarge.

Let us seek the unity of all sections of the Republic through
the prevalence in all of mutual respect, through the assurance
in all of local freedom, through the mastery in all of that
supreme spirit which flashed from the lips of Patrick Henry
when he said, in the first Continental Congress, "I am not a
Virginian, but an American." Let us take care that labor
maintains its ancient place of privilege and honor, and that

industry has no fetters imposed of legal restraint or of social discredit to hinder its work or to lessen its wage. Let us turn and overturn in public discussion, in political change, till we secure a civil service, honorable, intelligent, and worthy of the land, in which capable integrity, not partisan zeal, shall be the condition of each public trust; and let us resolve that, whatever it may cost of labor and of patience, of sharper economy and of general sacrifice, it shall come to pass that, wherever American labor toils, wherever American enterprise plans, wherever American commerce reaches, thither again shall go as of old the country's coin—the American eagle, with the encircling stars and golden plumes!—*July 4th, 1876.*

RELIGIOUS CHARACTER OF THE AMERICAN PEOPLE.

WILLIAM M. EVARTS.

OUR estimate of the condition of this people at the close of a century—as bearing on the value and efficiency of the principles on which the Government was founded, in maintaining and securing the permanent well-being of a nation—would, indeed, be incomplete if we failed to measure the power and purity of the religious elements which pervade and elevate our society. One might as well expect our land to keep its climate, its fertility, its salubrity, and its beauty, were the globe loosened from the law which holds it in an orbit where we feel the tempered radiance of the sun, as to count upon the preservation of the delights and glories of liberty for a people cast loose from religion, whereby man is bound in harmony with the moral government of the world.

It is quite certain that the present day shows no such solemn absorption in the exalted themes of contemplative piety as marked the prevalent thought of the people a hundred years ago; nor so hopeful an enthusiasm for the speedy renovation of the world as burst upon us in the marvelous and wide system of vehement religious zeal, and practical good works,

4*

in the early part of the nineteenth century. But these fires are less splendid, only because they are more potent, and diffuse their heat in well-formed habits and manifold agencies of beneficent activity. They traverse and permeate society in every direction. They travel with the outposts of civilization, and outrun the caucus, the convention, and the suffrage.

The church, throughout this land, upheld by no political establishment, rests all the firmer on the rock on which its founder built it. The great mass of our countrymen to-day find in the Bible—the Bible in their worship, the Bible in their schools, the Bible in their households—the sufficient lessons of the fear of God and the love of man, which make them obedient servants to the free Constitution of their country, in all civil duties, and ready with their lives to sustain it on the fields of war. And now, at the end of a hundred years, the Christian faith collects its worshipers throughout our land, as at the beginning. What half a century ago was hopefully prophesied for our far future, goes on to its fulfillment: "As the sun rises on a Sabbath morning and travels westward from Newfoundland to the Oregon, he will behold the countless millions assembling, as if by a common impulse, in the temples with which every valley, mountain, and plain will be adorned. The morning psalm and the evening anthem will commence with the multitudes on the Atlantic Coast, be sustained by the loud chorus of ten thousand times ten thousand in the Valley of the Mississippi, and be prolonged by the thousands of thousands on the shores of the Pacific."—*July 4th, 1876.*

THE SAFETY OF THE STATE.

I. N. TARBOX, D.D.

THE little springs, the sparkling rills,
    In lonely coverts hide ;
They run among the ancient hills,
    And through the shadows glide ;

Their birth is in the wilderness ;
From mountain wilds they go,
By many winding paths, to cheer
The thirsty lands below.

God guards the little mountain springs,
Nor lets their channels dry ;
He hovers on his cloudy wings
From out the stormy sky ;
He gives the rain and " snow like wool,"
And feeds this ceaseless flow,
To make the lowlands beautiful,
And waving harvests grow.

The strength that makes a nation great
In secret is supplied ;
The energies that build the State
In humble virtues hide ;
From simple homes among the hills
The primal forces flow,
The strength that conquers earthly ills,
And overcomes the foe.

And if these lonely fountains fail,
And little streamlets dry,
No art or cunning can avail ;
The nation's self must die ;
But if the mountain streams are pure,
And constant in their flow,
The nation's heritage is sure
In all the plains below.
                    —*The Congregationalist.*

CENTENNIAL HYMN.

WILLIAM CULLEN BRYANT.

THROUGH storm and calm the years have led
  Our nation on from stage to stage,
A century's space, until we tread
  The threshold of another age.

We see there, o'er our pathway swept,
  A torrent stream of blood and fire ;
And thank the ruling Power who kept
  Our sacred league of States entire.

O checkered train of years ! farewell,
  With all thy strifes and hopes and fears ;
But with us let thy memories dwell,
  To warn and lead the coming years.

And thou, the new-beginning age,
  Warned by the past, and not in vain,
Write on a fairer, whiter page
  The record of thy happier reign.
            —*Sung in New York, July 4th, 1876.*

PROGRESS IN THE CONDITIONS OF WELFARE AND HAPPINESS.

HENRY WARD BEECHER.

IN this country, during the last hundred years, the art of
living healthily has advanced immensely. Though cities have
enlarged, and though the dangers to sanitary conditions are
multiplied, science has kept pace with these dangers, and
there never was a time—I will not say in our own history, but
in the history of any nation on the globe—when the conditions
of life were so wholesome, the conditions of happiness so uni-
versally diffused, as they are to-day in this great land. We

grumble—we inherit that trait from our ancestors ; we often vex ourselves with melancholy prognostications concerning this or that danger. Some men are born to see the devil of melancholy ; they would see him sitting in the very door of heaven, methinks. Not I ; for though there be mischiefs and troubles, yet, when we look at the great conditions of human society, we shall find that they never were so favorable as they are to-day. More than that : if you will look at the diversity of the industries in which men ply their hands, if you look at the accumulating power of the average citizen, you will find that a man may earn more in a single ten years to-day than his ancestors could earn in the whole of their lives.

The heavens are nearer to us than to them, for we have learned the secrets of the storm and the sweep of the lightning. The world itself is but just outside our door. We can now call to Asia and the distant parts of the earth easier than New York could call to Boston or Philadelphia a hundred years ago ; all the fleets of the world bring hither the tribute of the globe, and that not for the rich man and the sumptuous liver, but for the common people of the land to which we all belong. The houses in which we live are better. The implements by which the common man works are multiplied ; the processes which he can control, and of which he gets the reflex benefit, are many and wide-reaching. And all that the soil has, and all that the sea has, and all that the mountain locks up, and all that is invisible in the atmosphere, are so many servitors working in this great democratic land for the multitude, for the great mass of the common people.

In that regard we are advanced far beyond the days of our fathers ; for they had not escaped from the hereditary notions, or aristocratic thoughts, the aristocratic classes, or the aristocratic tendencies even in government. But the progress of democracy—which is not merely political, but which is religious, in literature, art, even in mechanics—the wave of democratic influence has been for a hundred years washing in further and further toward the feet of the common people And to-day there is not on the face of the globe another

forty millions that have such amplitude of sphere, such
strength of purpose, such instruments to their hand, such
capital for them, such opportunity, such happiness.—*From
speech at Peekskill, July 4th, 1876.*

THE SONG OF 1876.

BAYARD TAYLOR.

WAKEN, voice of the land's devotion !
  Spirit of freedom, awaken all !
Ring, ye shores, to the song of ocean,
  Rivers answer and mountains call !
    The golden day has come ;
    Let every tongue be dumb
That sounded its malice or murmured its fears ;
    She hath won her story ;
    She wears her glory ;
We crown her the land of a hundred years !

Out of darkness and toil and danger
  Into the light of Victory's day,
Help to the weak and home to the stranger,
  Freedom to all, she hath held her way.
    Now Europe's orphans rest
    Upon her mother-breast ;
The voices of nations are heard in the cheers
    That shall cast upon her
    New love and honor,
And crown her the queen of a hundred years !

North and South, we are met as brothers ;
  East and West, we are wedded as one !
Right of each shall secure our mother's ;
  Child of each is her faithful son !
    We give thee heart and hand,
    Our glorious native land,

For battle has tried thee and time endears ;
    We will write thy story,
    And keep thy glory
As pure as of old for a thousand years !
      —*Sung at midnight, July 4th, 1876, in Union*
                Square, New York.

SAVE "THE OLD SOUTH."

WENDELL PHILLIPS.

THE consecration that the Puritans gave to these walls—to Christ, and the church—in 1729, is annulled. The ark of God has sought a new and perhaps a better shelter; but these walls received as real a consecration when Adams and Otis dedicated them to liberty. We do not come here to save the walls that have echoed to the prayers of Cotton and Prince and Eckley and the early saints of the colony. We come here to save the walls that echoed the sublime thought of Quincy when he said : " No matter where, nor how, nor for what cause, I mean to die a free man, and not a slave ! " As long as they stand, these arches will echo with the sublime and sturdy religious enthusiasm of Adams, with the unequaled eloquence of Otis, with Warren in his young genius and enthusiasm. I will not say it is a nobler consecration, I will not say that it is a better use ; I only say we come here to save what our fathers consecrated to the memories of the most successful struggle the race has ever made for the liberties of men.

What does *Boston* mean ? Since 1630 the living fiber that owns that name, running through history, means jealousy of power, unfettered speech, keen sense of justice, readiness to champion any good cause; that is the *Boston* Laud suspected, North hated, and the negro loved. If you destroy the scenes that perpetuate *that* Boston, then rebaptize her Cottontown, or Shoeville. Don't belittle these memories; they lie long hid, but only to grow stronger. You mobbed John Brown meet-

ings in 1860, and seemed to forget him in 1861 ; but the boys
in blue, led by that very mob wearing epaulets, marched from
State Street to the Gulf, because "John Brown's soul was
marching on." That and the flag—only two memories, two
" sentiments "—led the ranks.

. You spend half a million for a school-house. What school
so eloquent as these walls to educate citizens? Napoleon
turned his Simplon road aside to save a tree Cæsar had once
mentioned.   Won't you turn a street, or spare a quarter of an
acre to remind boys what sort of men their fathers were ?
Think twice before you touch these walls. We are only the
world's trustees. The Old South no more belongs to us than
Luther's, or Hampden's, or Brutus's name does to Germany,
England, or Rome. Each and all are held in trust as torch-
light guides and inspiration for any man struggling for
justice and ready to die for truth.

Make this forever a mechanics' exchange. Shelter the
mechanics under this roof ; consecrate it, in its original form,
to a grand public use for the common run of the people, the
bone and muscle. It will be the normal school of politics.
It will be the best civil-service reform agency that the
Republican party can adopt and use to-day. The influences
that linger in these old walls will forbid men to be the tools
of corruption or of tyranny. Once in their hands, neither
need, nor greed, nor the clamor for wider streets, will ever
desecrate what Adams and Warren and Otis made sacred
to the liberties of men.—*From Address in the Old South
Church, Boston, June 14th, 1876.*

THE OLD SOUTH CHURCH.

ABBIE H. MORRILL.

RING, Boston bells, ring out loud peals
    Far on the summer air,
And rouse the sons of liberty
    To save this house of prayer.

Our fathers built this honored pile
   In brave and olden days,
And gathered here to worship God
   With sound of prayer and praise.

These very walls are eloquent
   With voices of the past,
They tell the deeds our sires have done.
   Shall not the record last?

Though sound of British horse and foot
   Was heard along these aisles,
Oppression yielded to the right,
   And peace upon us smiles.

Our country boasts no castle old
   Or grand cathedral gray ;
And shall this brave historic shrine
   Be rudely torn away—

Torn from the hearts of those who hold
   Its sacred presence dear ?
No ! from New England hills resounds
   This answer loud and clear :

This landmark old, along the shore
   Of the receding past,
Shall shine out like a beacon-light
   Bright, cheering, and steadfast.

While onward roll the centuries,
   And brave and true our land,
A guard of right and liberty,
   Long may the " Old South " stand.

THE SCHOLAR IN POLITICS.

CHARLES KENDALL ADAMS.

THE hope of the country is in its higher education. The hope of our country is not solely, not even chiefly in our common schools, but largely in our colleges and universities. In every country truly free it is, after all, the cultivated mind that is the controlling influence and motor of affairs. Its operation may not be obvious, we may not see it, we may not feel it, we may not weigh it; but like one of the forces of nature, though it works silently, its potent influence is everywhere present. The force of gravity is so gentle that we can scarcely perceive it; and yet its millions of gossamer threads bind the earth together, and even keep the planets in their places.

Such is the influence of cultivated mind on society. Though Martin Luther began by begging his bread for a "pious canticle" in the streets of Eisenach, and though he was opposed by the opinions and the corruptions of his time; yet, by his studious toil of days and nights, he became able, as Lord Bacon said of him, "to summon all learning and all antiquity to his succor," and hence "was not only sustained by conquering armies and countenanced by princes, but, what was a thousand times better, was revered as a benefactor and a spiritual parent by millions of his grateful countrymen." I hold it to be the *duty*—I do not hesitate to use the strong old Saxon word—the *duty*, of every educator and of every seminary of higher learning to do what it can to modify the material tendencies of the age, both by precept and by example. I am persuaded that what the age needs, and what our nation is sighing for, is not so much a wider diffusion of the ability to read and write, as a higher standard of excellence, in morals and in intelligence and in learning, on the part of that class which creates and inspires and controls public opinion. A little learning may be better than no learning, but we must not forget that it becomes the "dangerous thing" of the proverb, when it only enables its possessor to lift himself into places of responsibility and power. Better lawyers, better physicians, better clergymen, better editors, better teachers, better legislators—these are the need of the republic, and it is only by producing these that we can make it certain that the republic will be better directed.—*June 27th, 1876.*

——————

JOHN A. ANDREW.

OLIVER WENDELL HOLMES.

BEHOLD the shape our eyes have known
Once more in changeless stone ;
So looked in mortal face and form
Our guide through peril's deadly storm.

But hushed the beating heart we knew,
That heart so tender, brave, and true ;
Firm as the rooted mountain rock ;
Pure as the quarry's whitest block.

Not his, beneath the blood-red star,
To win the soldier's envied scar ;
Unarmed he battled for the right
In duty's never-ending fight.

Unconquered, with unslumbering eye,
Faith such as bids the martyr die,
The Prophet's glance, the Master's hand
To mold the work his foresight planned—

These were his gifts : what Heaven had lent
For Justice, Mercy, Truth he spent ;
First to avenge the traitor's blow,
And first to lift the vanquished foe.

Lo ! thus he stood in danger's strait,
The pilot of the Pilgrim State.
Too large his fame for her alone ; .
The nation claims him as her own.
—*On unvailing a Statue of Gov. Andrew, Oct. 8th, 1875.*

DUTIES OF THE AMERICAN CITIZEN.

JOHN I. GILBERT.

WE are often told that republicanism, or popular government, is here on trial.   I tell you *no !*—a thousand times *no !*
It is we *ourselves* who are on trial—our fitness for self-government is being tested.   The principles of our government received their sanction when God created man in his own image,
free and rational.   The real question is : Shall that government be preserved and well administered ? Thomas Jefferson says : " The whole art of government consists in being
honest."

We, or our ancestors, have come from many different lands,
representing various political and religious creeds.   But *here*
we meet fraternally, and as Americans.   Let us unite in solv-
ing the remaining problems of social and individual life,
seeking not so much to promote our own views of truth as the
truth itself—the whole truth, and the truth of the whole.

In 1776 the *rights* of men were chiefly thought of.   The
supreme endeavor was to secure those rights.   In 1876 the
duties of citizenship should be of first concern.   Without sur-
rendering any of our rights, we should bend to the performance of duty.   The supreme need of the nation is citizen-
reform—a quickened conscience in public affairs.   The general demand for this is a good omen for the future.

As the republic itself is the product of a vital process—a
living growth—so the *purification* of the republic, its libera-
tion from all elements foreign and hostile to its spirit and
genius, must result from the growth of virtue in the private
citizen and in the public servant.   This can only be done by
all those influences and agencies by which individual character is formed.

Let us hope that on this centennial day the nation will drink
anew at the fountains of liberty and justice, of political wisdom
and public morality.   Let us catch the inspiration that comes
to us from all that is best and most heroic in the past.   As
we hail the dawn of the new century, let us be hopeful, but

not vainglorious. Let us cherish a rational yet ardent enthusiasm for the triumph of all that is good and true and beautiful in public and in private life.

Let us declare that this republic, born in the long agony of war, shall be first *pure*, then *peaceable*, and then *perpetual*. And for the support of *this* declaration, with a firm reliance on the continued aid of Divine Providence, shall we not mutually pledge to each other the devotion of our lives, our fortunes, and our sacred honor?—*From Address at Malone, N. Y., July 4th, 1876.*

----◆----

THE WORLD'S FAIR, 1876.

JAMES RUSSELL LOWELL.

COLUMBIA, puzzled what she should display
Of true home-make on her Centennial Day,
Asked Brother Jonathan : he scratched his head,
Whittled awhile reflectively, and said,
" Your own invention and own making, too ?
Why any child could tell ye what to do.
Show 'em your Civil Service, and explain
How all men's loss is everybody's gain ;
Show your new patent to increase your rents
By paying quarters for collecting cents ;
Show your short cut to cure financial ills,
By making paper-collars current bills ;
Show your new bleaching process, cheap and brief,
To wit : a jury chosen by the thief ;
Show your State Legislatures ; show your Rings ;
And challenge Europe to produce such things
As high officials sitting half in sight
To share the plunder and to fix things right ;
If that don't fetch her, why, you only need
To show your latest style in martyrs—Tweed ;
She'll find it hard to hide her spiteful tears
At such advance in one poor hundred years."

—The Nation.

RESISTANCE TO PARTY TYRANNY A DUTY.

WHITELAW REID.

WE do not have so many great men as formerly in public life. De Tocqueville explains the undeniable fact—far more conspicuous now, indeed, than in his time—by what he calls "the ever-increasing despotism of the majority in the United States." "This power of the majority," he continues, "is so absolute and irresistible that one must give up his rights as a citizen, and almost abjure his qualities as a man, if he intends to stray from the track which it prescribes." The declaration is extravagant ; yet who that has seen the ostracism of our best men, for views wherein they were only in advance of their times, will doubt that the tyranny of party and the intolerance of independent opinion among political associates constitute at once one of the most alarming symptoms of our politics, and one of the evils of our society to be most strenuously resisted ? We deify those who put what we think into fine phrases ; we anathematize those who, thinking the opposite, put it into equally fine phrases ; and we crucify those whom we have deified, when they presume to disagree with us. Is it needful, on New England soil, to look far for an illustration ? The Great New England senator, whose fame is a national honor, as his work is the national heritage, and who, as a foremost example of American scholarship applied to American politics, may fairly count on generous regard from an audience like this—whatever its partisan predilections,—who here needs to be reminded of what befell him, when, without stain on his character or change in his principles, he came to honest difference in opinion from the generation he had educated and the party he had helped to create ? Or take an earlier shame, and one that comes nearer to a New England college. Who here has forgotten how the very party which had hailed him prophet, turned to rend the first judicial officer of the nation, because, neither degrading his high place by apologies, nor yielding to partisan demands, he manfully did his duty in a great State trial ? He never did a higher duty. No citizen can do a higher duty than to resist the majority, when he believes it wrong ; to assert the right of individual judgment and maintain it ; to cherish liberty of thought and speech and action, against the tyranny of his own or any party. Till that tyranny—yearly growing more burdensome, as the main object of an old party becomes more and more the retention or the regaining of power, instead of the success of the fresh, vivid principles on which new parties are always organized—till that tyranny is in some measure broken, we shall get few questions considered on their merits, and fail, as we are failing, to bring the strongest men into the service of the state. Here, then, is another task in our politics, for which the scholar is peculiarly fitted by the liberality and independence to which he has been trained; and we may set it down as another of the functions whose discharge we have the right to expect at his hands : *To resist the tyranny of party and the intolerance of political opinion, and to maintain actual freedom as well as theoretical liberty of thought.* —*From Address at Amherst College, July 9th, 1873.*

WANTED—A MAN.

BY J. G. HOLLAND.

GOD give us men ! a time like this demands
Strong minds, great hearts, true faith, and ready hands.
Men whom the lust of office does not kill ;
Men whom the spoils of office cannot buy ;
Men who possess opinions and a will ;
Men who have honor ; men who will not lie ;
Men who can stand before a demagogue,
And damn his treacherous flatteries without winking ;
Tall men, sun crowned, who live above the fog
In public duty and in private thinking.
For, while the rabble with their thumb-worn creeds,
Their large professions, and their little deeds,
Mingle in selfish strife, lo ! Freedom weeps,
Wrong rules the land, and waiting Justice sleeps.

WOMEN IN POLITICS.

JOHN QUINCY ADAMS.

THE gentleman says that women have no right to petition on political subjects ; that it is discreditable, not only to their section of the country, but also to the national character ; that these females could have a sufficient field for the exercise of their influence in the discharge of their duties to their fathers, their husbands, or their children—cheering the domestic circle, and shedding over it the mild radiance of the social virtues, instead of rushing into the fierce struggles of political life. I admit, sir, that it is their duty to attend to these things. . . . But I say that the correct principle is, that women are not only justified, but exhibit the most exalted virtue, when they do depart from the domestic circle, and enter on the concerns of their country, of humanity, and of their God. . . . Why, sir, what does the gentleman understand by " political subjects " ? Everything in which this house has an agency ; everything which relates to peace and war, or to any of the great interests of society. Are women to have no opinions or actions on subjects relating to the general wel-fare ? Where did the gentleman get this principle ? Did he find it in Sacred History—in the language of Miriam the prophetess, in one of the noblest and most sublime songs of triumph that ever met the human eye or ear ? Did the gen-tleman never hear of the deed of Jael, who slew the dreaded enemy of her country ? Has he forgotten Esther, who, by *her petition*, saved her people and their country ? Sir, I might go through the whole Sacred History and find innumerable examples of women, who not only took an active part in the politics of their times, but who are held up with honor to posterity for doing so. . . .

And what were the women of the United States in the struggle of the Revolution ? Were they devoted exclusively to the duties and enjoyments of the fireside ? When the soldiers were destitute of clothing, or sick, or in prison, from whence did relief come ? From the hearts where Patriotism erects her favorite shrine, and from the hand that is seldom withdrawn when the soldier is in need. The voice of our history speaks, trumpet-tongued, of the daring and intrepid spirit of patriotism burning in the bosoms of the women of that day. . . . And, sir, is that spirit to be charged here, in this hall where we are sitting, as being "discreditable" to our country's name? So far from regarding such conduct as a national reproach, I approve of it, and I glory in it!

COLUMBIA'S ALOE.

MRS. M. B. C. SLADE.

THE Aloe drinks the sun and rain,
Nor blooms her answer back again
Till, lo ! a flowery crown she wears,
Sole blossom of an hundred years.
With rugged growth, from virgin soil,
Through vigorous effort, care, and toil,
With sturdy fiber, stock of strength,
With leaf of green, and limb of length,
See, now, Columbia's Aloe rise
And spread its branches to the skies !
Grand monarch of the New World's wood,
Its century's finished work is good.
Now wait we some consummate flower
To crown with grace such growth of power ;
The germ, the opening bud, we see ;
What marvel shall the blossom be ?
Fall, gentlest dew ; smile, sunbeam warm ;
Blow, strengthening gale ; rise, trying storm ;
Till blooms o'er all Columbia's heights
The Aloe flower of Woman's Rights.

—*From N. E. Journal of Education.*

CENTENNIAL BELLS.

BY FANNY FOSTER JENKINS.

HEAR the bells !
Midnight bells !
On the calm of night their music swells ;
Hushed the crowds upon the street, every heart-beat is a prayer,
As they listen to the chimes singing praises in the air,
At the turn of the year.

Hear the bells !
Freedom bells !
Since a hundred years their echo dwells
In the heart of freedom's sons. 'Tis that peal the people hear
That, a hundred years ago, greeted first the list'ning ear,
Proclaiming liberty.

Hear the bells !
Honor bells !
From many a tower their music wells ;
First in war and first in peace, to his duty ever true ;
Never let his praises cease, honor still where honor's due !
Far and wide, ring the bells !

Hear the bells !
Pealing bells !
Of a nation's joy their music tells !
God our Lord has led us on, kept us through a hundred years ;
Floods of joy our bosoms swell, fill our eyes with grateful tears.
Ring the bells ! ring the bells !

THE END.

www.ingramcontent.com/pod-product-compliance
Lightning Source LLC
Chambersburg PA
CBHW031441270326
41930CB00007B/817